BRIGHT IDEAS

Inspirations for THE INDEPENDENT READER

Published by Scholastic
Publications Ltd,
Villiers House,
Clarendon Avenue,
Leamington Spa,
Warwickshire CV32 5PR

©1992 Scholastic Publications Ltd

Written by Diana Bentley, Dee
Reid and Sylvia Karavis
Edited by Stella Paskins and
Christine Lee
Designed by Micky Pledge
Series designed by Juanita
Puddifoot
Illustrated by Linzi Henry
Cover design by Lynne Joesbury
Cover artwork by Ann Johns
Artwork by Steve Williams
& Associates, Leicester

Designed using Aldus Pagemaker
Processed by Studio Photoset,
Leicester.
Printed in Great Britain by
Ebenezer Baylis & Son, Worcester

British Library Cataloguing in Publication Data
A catalogue record for this book is available from the British Library

ISBN 0-590-53023-2

CONTENTS

Introduction

'Reading is much more than the decoding of black marks upon a page: it is a quest for meaning and one which requires the reader to be an active participant.' (DES/WO, 1989a)

By the age of seven most children have made a promising start with reading.

Their early years' experiences have taught them the pleasures and the skills inherent in reading. The challenge facing the teacher in the junior years is developing these children into confident and competent independent readers.

Although all children will have made progress since their first days of reading, it is inevitable that in every class there will be a wide range of differing abilities and enthusiasms.

BACKGROUND

Characteristics of readers in Y3 to Y6

The avid reader

Children who fall into this category usually display some, if not all, the following characteristics:
• The child seizes the opportunity to read in 'spare time';
• The child talks about favourite authors;
• The child is prepared to try new authors;
• The child reads from a wide range of texts – from comics to encyclopaedias;
• The child is eager to share responses about books;
• The child becomes totally immersed in the book during silent reading time;
• The child uses both the library and the book corner intelligently;
• The child knows he is a good reader.

Such children appear to need very little support from the teacher, but these promising characteristics can only too easily decline if they are not carefully nurtured. One of the dangers that may arise is that because these children are able to identify quickly what they find enjoyable, it can be difficult to entice them to explore other reading experiences. For some avid readers their interest lies exclusively with fiction, while others are hooked on information reading. Both groups need the opportunity and encouragement to read from a wide range of genres and not to become so expert in one aspect that they scorn other important forms of reading.

It is all too easy to expect these readers to be entirely self-sufficient and to fail to notice when they need help with book selection or to neglect to praise them when they have coped with a new challenge.

The struggling reader

Unfortunately, some children reach Y3 still very uncertain about the reading process. Some of these children will undoubtedly require specialist help. These children are still at the beginning stages of reading and will need the strategies and support normally given to the five-year-old (see D. Bentley et al, *Inspirations for Becoming a Reader*, Scholastic Publications Ltd, 1992).

There are other strugglers who are less obvious, who can decode simple print but who derive little pleasure from their reading experiences and who quickly label themselves as 'poor readers'.

Characteristics of the struggling reader are that:
• the child shows little interest in books and reading;
• the child is over-dependent on surface skills;
• the child rarely seeks for meaning when reading;
• the child finds it difficult to predict text;
• the child has developed many avoidance tactics when asked to read;
• the child increasingly relies on peers and friends to interpret texts;
• the child rarely makes any spontaneous comments while reading about the text;
• the child becomes increasingly embarrassed about the appearance of the books she is able to read.

There is a temptation for the teacher to spend considerably more time with these readers and to be continually asking to hear them read in the hope that this will give them the fluency they so obviously lack. However, although these children do need lots of reading experience, drawing attention to their problems by singling them out does not necessarily produce the desired result. It may be more productive to spend time boosting their self-image, by responding to them in the same way as we respond to the more able readers in the class, focusing on books they have read and the enjoyment they have got from them. If their only reading experience is falteringly reading aloud to their teacher, this only serves to remind them of what they cannot do.

Reading aloud is an important part of the diagnostic process, but if it is used exclusively then problems arise.
• It is very difficult for the teacher (and the child) to notice any progress. It is like trying to take measurements of a child's physical growth too frequently; progress can seem non-existent. It is better to make assessments of progress regularly but less frequently, then both teacher and pupil can take pride in any achievements.

• The child's reading experience is predominantly one of disappointment and failure.
• The child misses out on many of the more pleasurable aspects of reading, such as browsing through books, talking about books and sharing books with friends.

These children need achievable goals and lots of praise when they reach them. They need to be able to see the progress they are making and to believe that they will become readers.

It is vital to establish a good working relationship with the struggling reader. Too often teachers can allow the relationship to be dominated by improving reading skills, failing to notice that the child's enthusiasm for reading may be evaporating.

The take-it-or-leave-it reader

These children can read but often show little interest in doing so. They have mastered the decoding skills but have not yet become self-motivated and enthusiastic readers. Typically, these children will read to order but are unlikely to do so voluntarily or to take pleasure in exploring books. Reading is low on their list of optional priorities!

Characteristics of the 'take-it-or-leave-it' reader are that:
• the child is easily distracted from reading;
• the child is reluctant to try new authors or genres;
• the child may have a measure of competence in fiction reading but little ability to extract meaning from a non-fiction text, or vice-versa;
• the child lacks reading stamina. If the book does not offer immediate appeal the child rejects it. He is easily discouraged by such features as small print, too few illustrations or too many pages;
• the child shows little interest in talking about what he has read and rarely comments on book contents.

These children need considerable teacher support: they have the potential to be avid readers but without teacher intervention they may all too easily become struggling readers.

All children, whatever their ability, deserve the best resources a school can afford. They need experiences with books that are both challenging and satisfying and they need continual praise and encouragement if they are to become truly independent readers.

CHAPTER 1

Book resources in the classroom

Children need quick and ready access to book resources and, in order to provide this, most primary classrooms have a 'book corner' which is available to the whole class. Obviously no book corner will provide sufficient resources for all the children all of the time and 'libraries' or library-like corridors which contain a wider and more prolific number of books are also necessary (see Chapter 2, 'The school library').

However, classroom resources that are immediately to hand are more likely to be used on a regular and rapid basis. There are numerous occasions during a school day when some form of quick reference is needed. This may range from checking a spelling in a dictionary to finding a reference for a drawing, or from verifying a fact to trying to find an answer to a question. Catering for such diverse needs can be a major headache. The breadth of reading ability within any class, coupled with the need to ensure that all children are regularly exposed to every kind of reading matter, means that teachers have to select these resources very carefully.

BACKGROUND

Most pupils turn to fiction for the largest part of their 'free choice' reading time and almost all classes are likely to have a few titles by the really popular authors. Although the primary aim of fiction books is enjoyment, children should be encouraged to branch out and try other genres, other authors and other settings. Frequently this means careful preparation by the class teacher. This could be through reading to the class from a wide range of authors, or it could be by selecting short passages to read aloud as a 'taster' for the children. Coupled with encouraging children to look at the blurb on the covers of books, this careful preparation can form a strong launching pad and provide sufficient enticement for readers to persevere with a new author (see Chapter 3, 'Reading fiction').

Children should also be encouraged to read non-fiction (see Chapter 4, 'Reading non-fiction'). These books should be given careful consideration when choosing books for the classroom. Since many children do not find the prospect of reading non-fiction books as attractive as reading fiction, such titles should be chosen carefully for their reading value, rather than to support an ongoing topic or project.

As adults, we read an amazing number of different texts, which require different reading styles, and this range should be reflected in a book corner. The following list is by no means exhaustive but it will help to clarify the kinds of reading genres to which children also need to be introduced.

Annuals
These are very popular because they offer a variety of short reading material that children can dip into.

Atlases
A rule of thumb is to select the largest, clearest and most informative one that will not cause a major storage problem. With the increased emphasis upon geography in the primary school, there is now a wide range to choose from that have been produced specifically for younger readers.

Autobiographies/biographies

There are short biographies suitable for this age group, eg. those which describe the lives of sport and television personalities.

Children's classics

These are frequently chosen as 'read-aloud' texts, but many of them require several weeks to complete and children may find it very difficult to sustain their interest. (See 'Taped stories', page 13, as an alternative way of introducing these texts.)

Diaries

This is an increasingly popular form of writing. The diary's short entries and personal comments seem to appeal to readers of all ages and abilities.

Dictionaries

Most classrooms have junior dictionaries available for class or group activities, but in the reference section of the book corner a large adult dictionary is invaluable. The greatest use a dictionary receives in the primary years is undoubtedly for checking spelling. A traditional dictionary is not necessary for this task and, indeed, all the extra information provided tends to make the task take longer. Spelling dictionaries are cheaper and more practical. However, the primary function of a dictionary is to extend and clarify the meanings of words and therefore a large dictionary with all the definitions and guides to pronunciation needs to be introduced to the children. It is essential that children should not only be shown the use of such a dictionary, but also that they should be shown *how* to read it. Too often the able reader rushes at the definition, trying to 'read' the words as though they were part of a novel, and is consequently unable to make sense of the explanation.

Encyclopaedias

Although these are more likely to be found in the school library, the single-volume editions written for the younger reader are a valuable classroom resource and prevent too many protracted visits to the library. Again, you need to demonstrate how to use the various forms of encyclopaedias. Some are arranged alphabetically, others divide the contents into broad subject bands, such as 'People' or 'Animals'. Many provide guide words at the top of the pages and the value of these should be pointed out to the children.

Fables/animal stories

These are very popular with less confident readers, possibly because the challenges they offer in the 'moral' interpretation frequently lead to much discussion and book talk.

Folk tales/fairy tales

It is sometimes assumed that these are only suitable for the infant years. However, this genre gives the scope for exploring many important themes and issues. The universality of these tales means they are an ideal medium for exploring cross-cultural literature.

Friends' writing/teachers' writing

Placing home-made books alongside published materials increases their status and offers children an opportunity to read each other's work over a long period of time. All too often sharing writing takes place immediately after the completion of the piece and is quickly forgotten by both author and friend. Children need to see models of writing done by peers. Just as students often consult each other's dissertations in order to get the feel of what is required, so pupils should be allowed to consult and constructively criticise the work of their peers. A glossy, published book generally appears too authoritative to criticise and often any criticism offered takes the form of 'It is boring' or 'I didn't like it'. With peer group writing this changes to 'Why didn't you...?' or 'Did you think...?'

Humorous books/joke books

The brevity of these kinds of texts appeals to many young readers and as they enjoy the puns they gain important insight into the versatility of language.

Historical novels

These offer the reader a chance to experience 'history' through narrative which may bring alive a period of history.

Information leaflet

A collection of these can form a very useful resource that needs only cost 'time' as so many leaflets are available free of charge. A visit to the local tourist office, travel agency, doctors' surgery and supermarket will provide a wide variety of formats and reading levels.

Instruction books

These are frequently overlooked as a resource, but in fact form an important part in most children's reading. Reading instruction requires practice – a slow careful read is demanded by these texts and many children need to be shown how to intepret them.

Letters

There are a number of books which use the 'letter' format to unfold the story. They are valuable for showing two points of view of the same events.

Magazines

Magazines form a large part of most adult reading and children also enjoy the chance to dip in and out of such literature. Generally children can be depended upon to provide those magazines which support their hobbies, but magazines about children's books (such as *Books for Keeps*) can also be included. Children may well alert you to an interesting book to consider for the book corner after they have browsed through these.

Newspapers

Although newspapers become dog-eared very quickly, they are worth considering for inclusion in the book corner. There are now many newspapers aimed specifically at the young reader. The task of removing old and tatty newspapers could be part of the book corner monitor's responsibility.

Novels of all kinds

These need to range across the following genres – mystery, adventure, school, science fiction, fantasy, choose your own adventure, animal stories, true life adventures.

Myths/legends

These powerful tales appeal to many upper juniors who relish the moral issues they pose.

Plays

Play reading in small groups offers children a chance to share and discuss their responses and explore character through dialogue and actions.

Poetry

This should range from amusing simple light verse to longer narrative poems.

Taped stories

Many children find the prospect of reading 'classic' books too daunting and too demanding for their reading ability, so listening to high quality taped versions is an excellent alternative. These are sometimes available in abridged form, but a full reading of the book is far more satisfactory. In many cases, such tapes have provided the necessary stimulus and confidence for children to try

the texts afterwards – in the same way that televising a book has been shown to increase book sales dramatically.

Thesaurus

These are now available for young junior readers and provide opportunities for them to consider the diversity of language.

Timetables

These require a specific reading skill which needs to be practised in the classroom.

Travel books

Many children are interested in the wider world and these stories give the reader a feeling of 'experiencing' countries they are unlikely to have visited.

How long will this book last with class 3b?

Other books in this series include CARS TRAINS AEROPLANES HELICOPTERS BIKES

BOATS

Criteria for selecting books

It would be wonderful to have the time to examine carefully and discuss every book and resource before committing the school to purchasing it. However, this is obviously impossible and teachers often need to make quick decisions or rely upon the publishers to have vetted the titles within a series for their uniform quality. The criteria below may help as guidelines for assessing individual titles. However, bear in mind that you will not have the time to apply every aspect to the books in your classroom. It is a good idea to work with colleagues when trying to select resources for your school, and you may also find the children in your class to be a valuable source of information.

One school decided to capitalise on the perceptions of the older children in Y6 and asked them to evaluate all the new books that came into the school – including books for the reception class. They

became avid and discerning literary critics, and alerted teachers to problems as wide-ranging as difficult or distorted illustrations, down to weak spines and poor typefaces. A bonus of this exercise was that it gave the poorer readers among them a reason for reading simple texts and at the same time raised their self-esteem.

Literary, cultural and social qualities

• Is the book well written, with language that reads well aloud?
• Are the illustrations sympathetic to the text?
• Does the book genuinely enhance the self-image of children and adults from all cultures and backgrounds?
• Does the book avoid stereotyping?
• Is the information accurate and up-to-date?

• Will the book offer the satisfaction of having learned something about oneself or the world?

Assessing the physical attributes of books

• Is the cover of the book sufficiently attractive to entice the child to take it from the shelf?
• Is the binding sturdy enough for its potential use?
• Is the type size suitable and clear enough for the intended audience?
• Are there both hardback and paperback editions? If so, which is the better value for money?
• When was the book published? Is this likely to affect the information contained within the pages?

• If the book has been in the school for over five years and still seems in good condition, is it because it is not being borrowed or used?

Taking a good look at the resources

Expanding a book collection with new publications is obviously desirable, but there is also a need to 'weed' periodically.

This is best done at the end of term when all the books are together, rather than during the term when so many may be in drawers or at home. Books that are tatty and dirty make an obvious choice but you need to consider the popularity of the other titles available. Maybe some books are in good condition because they are not being selected. Is it because they do not reflect the interest of the class? Is the text dull, difficult or insufficiently informative? It may be that some such books could be of more value in another classroom, or in the library.

It is always difficult to reject a book outright. There is a story of one school who asked for help from an education library in pruning their books. This was duly given and, after a morning's work, a large pile of old and outdated books was placed in the staffroom. The librarian asked the staff to approve her selection and added that staff could take back any they wished to keep – the rest she would dispose of. She returned to find only two books left – the others had all been reprieved! You may well need to be ruthless to restrict choice to quality rather than quantity.

ACTIVITIES

1. Getting to know the books

Age range
Seven to eleven.

Group size
Two to six children.

What you need
A wide selection of reading material in the book corner.

What to do
Select a group of two to six children and ask them to be responsible for organising the book corner for a week. Discuss with them the need to select a number of 'featured' books each week. These could be books on a specific topic, or books by a certain author. Alternatively, they could be selected purely on a basis of personal choice. These books can be displayed and changed as the group decides over one week. This should mean that every child has at least one week in a year when he is responsible for the books.

Ensure that the group responsible keeps the area attractive and well organised (for example, the books displayed in author order, the non-fiction books together under subjects, the magazines, brochures and comics neatly stacked in the appropriate box). Encourage the children to arrange the furniture themselves, deciding on the best place for the tape-recorder and where to place the cushions.

Ask the book monitors to select and talk about their 'books of the week' as their turn comes to an end. Encourage them either to read short extracts of text or to give a brief outline of why they chose a particular book.

Some schools regularly exchange the books between the library and the classroom, and a rota of books is likely to make the book choice more attractive. Allow the monitors to make a personal choice of ten to twenty books from the library at the beginning of their term of office, and to select a similar number to be returned at the same time. This will ensure a continuous turnover. However, before returning titles, ask the monitors to let the class know which ones are being sent back in case a child has been waiting for one of the books to become available.

2. The five-finger choice

Age range
Any age.

Group size
Individuals.

What you need
Any books with over 100 words per page.

What to do
Matching a child with a book needs careful consideration (see Chapter 12, 'Hearing children read'). Johnson (1973) suggests a method that children can use quickly to check whether a book is likely to be too difficult.

Ask the child to open the book somewhere near the middle and to start reading. When he comes to a word he does not know, ask him to put his little finger on it, then put his fourth finger on the next word he does not know, and so on. Explain that if all five fingers are used up on that page, the book is likely to be too difficult for him, or that he should seek help with it.

This is based on the idea that anything over five unknown words in a hundred will cause frustration for a reader. Some teachers feel that even this is too difficult for a child reading alone and suggest only one word per hundred.

3. Making a class dictionary

Age range
Any age.

Group size
Small group to whole class, working in pairs.

What you need
Whiteboard, paper, card, dictionary for reference.

What to do
Explain to the group that they are going to make a dictionary associated with a topic. Ask the children to give you as many words as they can think of associated with that subject. Write the words on the board. With the help of the group, place the words in alphabetical order.

Ask the children to form pairs, then give each pair a word from the board. Explain that they now have to write a dictionary definition for that word (if possible without referring to a published dictionary). Let them compare their definition with the published dictionary definition when they have finished. Continue until all the words have been defined.

Let the children then write out their definition on to paper and explain that this is now going to go into a class book for the book corner. Ask the children to select guide words for the top of the pages. Suggest that they identify the part of speech and any other features that they think would be useful. Bind the book and place it in the book corner.

This activity can be very useful for projects, and for developing an understanding of mathematical terms, parts of speech and so on.

4. What do we read in a week?

Age range
Seven to eleven.

Group size
Individuals.

What you need
Pencil, paper.

What to do
Ask the children to keep a list for one week of all the different kinds of reading they do, for example, cereal packets, television advertisements, road signs and so on. Turn the activity into a competition to see who has read the most widely.

One teacher brought in to the classroom all the reading she did in a day, demonstrating both the value and need to read, as well as the wide variety of reading which is done every day. Her reading material included a bedtime book, a newspaper, the medical instructions on a packet of pills, a recipe, free offer mail, a computer manual, video instructions, the children's stories and so on.

5. What is being borrowed?

Age range
Seven to eleven.

Group size
Whole class.

What you need
Either a detachable adhesive label or a sheet of paper placed inside each book.

What to do
Ask the monitors to place the paper or label inside the cover of each book on the shelves. For one month ask the children in the class to tick the piece of paper each time they refer to, or borrow any book.

At the end of this time divide the books out among the class. Ask the children to write down the title of the books they examine and to add the marks up. Using their results, display a list of the top twenty books that have been borrowed.

Ask the class why they think the bottom twenty books were not borrowed. (Perhaps these should be removed from the collection.)

CHAPTER 2

The school library

'At their best, school libraries offer pupils the resources that study requires: access to reference books, information in different forms, a place to read socially. Children who learn to browse amongst books, newspapers and magazines, glancing, page turning, pursuing ideas or idling, come to be at home in a library.' (Margaret Meek, 1991).

As the above quotation suggests, children who have easy and frequent access to a well-stocked library come to know that it is a lively and interesting place. They learn that it is a place where specific information may be found, that ideas and opinions may be explored there and that time spent 'just browsing' there is pleasurable. The library should be an integral part of the school. All too often children visit the library only in the course of topic work. As a result many children view the library and its contents rather like a museum – something to visit occasionally and sometimes to write about!

In order to ensure that the library and its resources are used effectively, staff should develop a whole policy for the library. Criteria for selecting and maintaining the stock and a system for managing it should be agreed by all members of staff and the following questions should be addressed:
• Should both fiction and non-fiction be included in the school library?
• How should the library be organised?
• When should books be discarded?
• Who will be responsible for the day-to-day appearance of the library area/room?

BACKGROUND

Organisation

There are many different ways of organising a school library. Some schools colour code all the books in order to help the children select more confidently. The school library offers an opportunity for even very young children to learn how a 'real' library works. If children become used to looking for fiction under alphabetically arranged authors, and non-fiction arranged according to the Dewey system or arranged in a way that reflects the Dewey categories, they will learn to use other libraries with confidence. Of course, children will sometimes need help and guidance. If possible there should always be someone on hand to help, maybe a parent, an older pupil or the teacher. If it is difficult to organise full-time support, it may be worth considering arranging and publicising 'opening hours' when extra help will be available in the library. Above all, the children need to think of a library as somewhere for them, where they can find books, a relaxed atmosphere and resources that they will enjoy.

Stock

Every book in the library should be of a quality and condition that justifies a place on the shelves. The book stock needs to be constantly reviewed. If the books are not regularly and systematically reviewed, there is a danger that the children will not be able to 'see the wood for the trees', in which case new additions might become 'lost' inside a dated collection.

Criteria for choosing book

As far as possible the library stock should include:
• good quality fiction for all the pupils whatever their reading level;
• good quality non-fiction that uses both photographic and drawn illustrations;
• different texts offering a wide variety of reads, including poetry, riddles, jokes, comics, newspapers, fiction, non-fiction, biographies, etc;
• books that have a wide variety of good illustrations – from cartoons to oil paintings;
• a wide variety of wordless and picture books for children of all ages;
• some dual language texts of quality stories and non-fiction.
  Books should contain:
• language that is memorable and that does not read in a contrived or unnatural way;
• texts that promote reflection or discussion to which the reader will want to return;

• texts that are non-racist and that do not demean people from any nationality, race or creed.

Books with torn covers or pages missing need to be renovated or removed. Out-dated non-fiction books containing inaccurate information need to be weeded out periodically. You may well consider obtaining multiple copies of popular titles, and remove old, unread titles that are only taking up valuable space.

Furnishing

The library, like the class book corner, needs to be a bright and enticing area with clearly labelled sections. If possible, furnish part of the library with floor cushions, bean bags or low chairs where children can sit and relax, or where they can comfortably read a few pages of one or two books before making their final choice. Another area could be made into a 'listening post' with headphones, easy-to-use tape-recorders and with a range of tapes stored nearby. A work area with tables, chairs and good lighting is essential and, if possible, this should be near the non-fiction material.

Displays

Many children have little experience of visiting or using a library. Indeed, some children regard the library merely as a 'room where books are stored', so the contents and purpose need to be promoted. Displays of the work of particular authors and/or illustrators can do much to advertise things that can be found in the library, as can topic-related displays. Displays that reflect children's hobbies will encourage them to use the library and help them to appreciate how to use it for their own interests, as well as for the current class topic.

Responsibility for the organisation of displays and the general tidiness of the library could be shared between all the classes in the school. During the period that a class is on 'library duty', all the children in the class could be responsible for deciding which themes or topics should be featured in the displays. Each child in that class could then be asked to contribute something towards the display such as a poster, jacket design or book review.

By being involved in the general upkeep of the library, children will learn how it is organised. This regular responsibility will help children to see that the library is an integral part of the school.

Giving certificates of merit to children who have contributed to the library is a popular means of encouraging interest. Awards could be made for such things as designing an 'eye-catching interest-raising' poster, for replacing misplaced books, or for having read ten books. A selection of appropriate certificates can be found on photocopiable pages 152 to 153.

Resources

Resourcing a library is expensive so a book-buying policy and regular stock reviews are important. The aim should be to have as wide a range of books as possible, with no one section being significantly larger than the other. For example, it would not be very useful to have twenty books on transport and just two on natural history. Obviously, some subjects are more widely written about than others, making choice relatively easy. On the other hand, it can be tempting to 'over-buy' at the expense of other subject areas.

A starting point for developing a whole-school book-buying policy could be for every class to be involved in a review of existing stock. Each class would be responsible for counting the number of books in one or more categories, checking publication dates and, in the case of non-fiction, whether or not the information is out of date.

Apart from the books, magazines and newspapers bought by the school, it is sometimes possible to increase the library's resources in other ways. Some families or individuals may be willing to give a book as a gift to the library when their child leaves the school. A local book shop might be willing to put on a display of books in school at the end of the summer term and several children may like to contribute towards a book for the library. Their names could be written inside the book as a memorial of their time in the school. There are also several school book clubs which run schemes whereby they give books to the school according to the number of books purchased by the children (see Resources, page 192).

Promoting the library

In addition to the suggestions made above, the library may be promoted in the following ways.

• Draw up a rota so that each class in school has a regular story reading session in the library. This could take the form of independent reading, an adult (parent, classroom assistant, teacher) reading to the children or children reading to children.

SUGGESTIONS BOOK
What would *you* like in our library?

Name	Suggestion
Abid P.	More softer chairs please
Sara Parker	Please can we get some more books about horses and...

• Feature particular authors or illustrators. Make a display of their work in the library and consider inviting them into school to talk to the children. If this cannot be arranged, you could perhaps show a video of an author or illustrator talking about how they set about writing and/or drawing. (Videos can be bought from The Children's Book Foundation, see Resources, page 192.)
• Form a library committee which could include a representative from each class, a member of staff and a parent librarian. This group could be responsible for such things as planning a timetable for classes to take turns in keeping the library tidy, organising displays, checking the suggestions book (see below) and, where possible, acting on the suggestions.
• Provide a suggestions book in the library and encourage the children to use it. They might like to request a particular book, ask for a display on a favourite theme or offer suggestions about the organisation of the furniture or stock. They may even offer to ask their parents to donate an old easy chair or cushion that is no longer wanted at home.
• Encourage every child to keep a 'Library Record'. This could be a part of their personal reading record or could be completely separate. The children could develop this book or folder to include a plan of the library, an annotated list of the Dewey numbering system or a page listing the books considered to be the most/least informative on a particular subject, including the reasons for their opinion. For example, the comments 'no index', 'would be better if diagrams were used to help explain the information', or 'good balance between text and illustration' could be used.
• Use assemblies to introduce new additions to the library, publicise forthcoming attractions, announce library competitions (see below) or commend the class currently responsible for the daily care of the library.
• Have regular competitions to encourage children to see the library as an interesting and lively place. For example, they could design a poster or book jacket, have a 'Readerthon' with a difference – held between classes rather than individuals, the winners being the class who has read the widest range of books. By organising the 'Readerthon' like this, even the children who see themselves as 'not very good at reading' can take part.

These activities can be used with the whole school and are intended to help children to see the library as an interesting and integral part of the school. By encouraging the children to participate in its organisation and running, they will come to feel at home there and recognise the pleasure and satisfaction that the library has to offer.

ACTIVITIES

1. Character quiz

Age range
Any age.

Group size
Pairs.

What you need
Library books, a selection of writing materials, a selection of drawing materials.

What to do
Ask the children to work with a partner to devise a character quiz. The character they choose must be from a library book that they have read or have heard read to them. Explain that they may elect either to write or draw their clues. They should not mention the title or author of the book, but must reveal their chosen character by describing or illustrating actions or appearance, particular expressions or sayings, or other characters in the story. For example, 'This person likes playing tricks and frequently tells lies, and has an aunt who likes going to the theatre.' (Answer: *Matilda – Who Told Lies and Burned to Death* by Hilaire Belloc.) Alternatively, a drawing might show a girl filling an entire room, or swimming in a pool with a mouse. (Answer: *Alice in Wonderland* by Lewis Carroll.)

When all the pairs have completed their character quiz, ask them to number and display them. Then invite other pairs to see how many characters and authors they can recognise.

2. Dewey pairs game

Age range
Nine to twelve years.

Group size
Two to four children.

What you need
Blank cards, copies of photocopiable page 154, pens.

What to do
Write each Dewey category number on a separate card. Write the category for each number on a matching card. (A list of the Dewey categories and their numbers can be found on photocopiable page 154.)

Allow the children to play Pelmanism with the cards.

Alternatively, let them play a pairs game by dealing five cards to each player and placing the rest of the pack face down in the centre of the table. Ask the players to check their hands for pairs of cards and, if they find any, to place them face up on the table in front of them. Ask the players then to take it in turn to remove a card from the pack. If a player can use the card to make a pair, ask her to place the new pair face up in front of her and discard one of the cards left in her hand, putting it to the bottom of the pile. If a player cannot make a pair but wishes to keep the card taken from the pile, ask her to discard another card. The first person to get rid of all of her cards is the winner.

3. Publicity poster

Age range
Any age.

Group size
Individuals or pairs.

What you need
Materials for making posters (large sheets of paper, paint, felt-tipped pens, adhesive, card, collage materials, etc).

What to do
Discuss with the children why the library should be publicised. Make a list of the suggestions that the children offer and ask them to use one or more of these as a basis for designing and making a poster.

When the posters are finished, display them in strategic places around the school.

4. Fact or fiction mobile

Age range
Any age.

Group size
Two to four children.

What you need
Card, cotton, thin cane or bamboo skewers (with the points removed), assortment of collage materials, felt-tipped pens, pencils, scissors, adhesive.

What to do
This activity encourages children to reflect on what they have read and to explore such things as relationships between characters, plot and setting, or what is relevant in an information book. Ask the groups of children each to think of a book (fiction or non-fiction) that they would really like to tell somebody else about. Let the groups discuss, then make a list of, the best, most interesting or most important things in that book. When the list is complete, ask them to double-check it to make sure that they have included only the most important or interesting things.

Explain that, using the list as their plan, they are going to make a mobile to tell others about their book. When the mobiles are finished hang them in the library, as near as possible to the place where the book is shelved.

Further activity
To extend this activity, ask children to conduct a survey on what effects the mobiles had on other library users. They could then use this information to help evaluate the degree of success their mobile had in giving information to others or attracting new readers.

5. Find a book, find a fact

Age range
Nine to twelve years.

Group size
Pairs.

What you need
Pencils, paper.

What to do
Ask each pair of children to select an information book and explain that they are to use the book to make up a quiz for another pair. Encourage them to use the contents and index pages to locate the information they wish to use in their quiz. Set a limit on the number of questions that they can ask – between three and five is probably enough to start with.

Slip the questions into the front of the relevant book.

Questions could be similar to the following:
• When did Mahatma Ghandi die? See page 35.
• When was the polaroid camera developed? See page 44.
• Find three new words that were introduced into the English language during the 1940s. See page 45.
• Which is the closest planet to the sun? See page 18.
• What do these abbreviations stand for: NB; sae; RSVP? See page 171.
• On what pages would you find information about butterflies?
• How many times is the thrush mentioned on page 26?

As the children write down their questions, ask them to write the answers on a separate piece of paper, making sure that each sheet is clearly labelled. Slip the answer sheet into the back of the book so that the children can check against these after they have attempted to answer the questions. Let the children swap quizzes with another pair. Alternatively, use the questions to make a 'questions and answers' resource in the library for anyone to use.

CHAPTER 3

Reading fiction

Many fluent readers aged eight and over have achieved their fluency by reading stories. Indeed for some of them reading is synonymous with narrative fiction. But although many of these young readers have acquired a level of reading skill, they then appear to remain on a plateau, never developing into fully competent readers who tackle the challenge of more demanding fiction.

Typically, such pupils will choose from a very limited range of stories. Sometimes they will read only the books of one author and find it difficult to switch to another once the supply has been exhausted. What can be done to help these children develop into confident and competent readers with a varied reading diet? First of all, it is important to recognise which are the fluent readers, and which need further encouragement.

Characteristics of fluent readers

• Fluent readers have *swift eye movements* which enable them to move speedily along a line of print and back down to the next line accurately.
• Fluent readers have an *extensive sight vocabulary* which means that they can recognise the majority of words without hesitation and they only break down words into phonic segments when they meet a new long word.
• Fluent readers have a variety of *word attack skills*. They use a combination of different strategies to decode words and, more importantly, use these strategies automatically so that the reader is free to focus on meaning rather than decoding.
• Fluent readers *self-correct* quickly.
• Fluent readers understand both the surface meaning and the *inferential meaning*.
• Fluent readers *respond on a personal level* to what they have read – they 'live' in the book while they are reading it.
• Fluent readers *bring knowledge to each text* to assist interpretation and they take new ideas from books to increase their own knowledge. (adapted from *Independence in Reading* by Don Holdaway, Ashton Scholastic, 1972)

Choosing more demanding books

It is worth noting that many adult readers of fiction often have quite narrow interests. For example, they might read fiction generically termed 'romance' but would not choose anything classed as 'historical romance' and would never consider reading 'science fiction'. Personal preference is undoubtedly the reader's prerogative, but for children in Y4 to Y6 such narrow selection can be too limiting.

Another problem is that readers of this nature often choose books that make few challenges, either in terms of the concepts explored or the characters portrayed. The stories are, on the whole, lightweight and trivial, offering instant gratification for very little effort.

It would be unrealistic to expect children always to reject the easy read and select a book which will challenge them. Indeed, relaxation reading is very important. But

if this is the only reading children ever do, then books that require more demanding reading skills are unlikely to be appreciated.

There are several ways in which you can stimulate children to be more adventurous in their reading habits.

• Read aloud to the class. By reading aloud to children you can whet their appetite for more demanding books. (For a full discussion of the benefits of reading aloud, see Chapter 9, 'Reading aloud'.)

• Organise group reading sessions. Sharing a story with peers can often provide the motivation for children to persevere with a more demanding read, where the individual reader might just give up. (For an explanation of the 'how' and 'why' of group reading, see Chapter 7, 'Group reading'.)

• Keep a careful record of children's choices in fiction. This record can reveal the pattern of any individual's reading habits. It should be immediately obvious which children are content always to settle for the undemanding book. If you feel that a child might enjoy tackling a more difficult book, this could be introduced in a book talk or conferencing session where other children might offer insights and opinions about the book.

• Provide children with stories on cassette tapes. This is a very useful way to introduce children to longer and more demanding stories. They are also versatile as they can be used for a whole class activity, a group activity or by an individual using a headset.

Going beyond the 'safe read'

Children sometimes seem reluctant to branch out from very safe reading experiences. Undoubtedly one reason for this is the natural human inclination to be content with the familiar. It is also possible that children do not have access to a suitable environment which would encourage more challenging reading. Such books cannot be satisfactorily read in odd moments across the school day. They require a more extended reading period, such as would be provided in a USSR session (see Chapter 8, 'USSR').

What are the difficulties?

Traditionally, teachers have believed that what children find difficult with more demanding fiction is the vocabulary, that is, unfamiliar words. While it is perfectly true that these words may initially baffle the young reader, many Y4 to Y6 children are familiar with a range of strategies for decoding unfamiliar words. They are used to reading and rereading and making informed guesses, and frequently these strategies produce satisfactory results. However, children of this age are not so experienced at dealing with other aspects of a text. There are several factors that can come between the child and the comprehension of whatever he is reading.

Punctuation

Although it is true to say that most children could not manage even simple fiction if they did not have *any* understanding of the use of the full stop, they may not be as familiar with other features of punctuation such as brackets, colons and dashes, all of which contribute to conveying the author's ideas on paper. Ironically teachers of Y4 to Y6 often spend time teaching children to use punctuation correctly in their *writing*, but rarely focus upon its importance in understanding meaning in a book. Yet misreading or ignoring punctuation can be quite as serious an interruption in making sense of a passage as misreading any words. For example:

'So Kev went into the shop scared not wanting to yet keen to see this place full of books.'*

Without the correct punctuation this sentence is very difficult to comprehend, although most children would not have difficulty reading the words. It is important to look for danger signals – when children are satisfied if they have read all the words correctly, even if the sentence does not make sense to them. Children will often ask for help from a teacher or a peer if they cannot read a particular word, but few will ask for help in deciphering the sense. These skills of 'reading' punctuation should be part of the reading programme for newly fluent readers. It is not the text that is at fault if the child is not able to interpret the punctuation.

Pronouns

Some newly fluent readers lose their way in texts when they meet too many pronouns too quickly, particularly when the pronoun opens a subsequent paragraph. For example, in the sentence 'As she did not fall off her horse, Gillian realised she had become a more confident rider,' some children might find the forward reference to Gillian very difficult. However, most are

* 'So Kev went into the shop – scared, not wanting to, yet keen to see this place full of books.' Joan Aiken, *The Erl King's Daughter*, Heinemann Banana Books, 1988.

quite able to cope with a pronoun used in the same sentence as the noun to which it refers.

To help children to feel confident at attributing pronouns correctly it is best to set tasks based around real reading experiences. Children could work in pairs, using a story that they have both read, and identify the pronouns and to discuss which nouns they refer. They could also see what would happen if more pronouns were used, or more nouns. Link these activities to the children's own writing so that they can discuss them at the draft stage.

Irony

Some young readers find irony in texts very difficult to comprehend. This is because they are often satisfied with their initial interpretation of the words used, rather than searching for the meaning that the author intended. It's not a problem which crops up in television as it is often conveyed through tone of voice. For example, if the 'baddy' says, 'I am *so* pleased to see you,' it should be quite obvious that he means exactly the opposite.

Children can understand irony when it is made obvious in a picture book. Ruth Brown's book *Our Cat Flossie* (Beaver Books, 1987) does this very successfully. For example, the text says that Flossie the cat's hobbies include 'birdwatching and fishing'. The illustrations show her looking greedily at the budgie in the cage and with her paw in the garden pond ready to dab at the poor unsuspecting goldfish.

You can help children become familiar with irony by:
• regularly reading aloud, conveying meaning by your tone of voice;
• encouraging children to discuss books in groups, looking specifically for examples of irony;
• encouraging children to incorporate irony into their own writing.

Alternative meanings

Some young readers whose early reading experiences have been predominantly reading-scheme based, may find it difficult to grasp that words often have alternative meanings. They may be unfamiliar colloquial expressions, for example, 'He comes from a rum family' or 'Nora half-inched 50p from his pocket.' A good example of the slippery nature of language is the word 'wicked' which has a dictionary definition of 'wrong; immoral; spiteful' but is currently used by children to describe anything that is really good!

It is neither possible nor necessary to avoid books which might contain potentially ambiguous sentences, but it is important to discuss with children how texts are constructed, and how meanings are not always fixed and may be determined by context.

Recommended authors for children in Y3 to Y6

Y3 – Y4
Tony Bradman
Jeff Brown
Ann Cameron
Roald Dahl
Dick King-Smith
Sheila Lavelle
Chris Powling
David Thomson
Jill Tomlinson
Hazel Townson

Y5 – Y6
Bernard Ashley
Betsy Byars
Gillian Cross
Colin Dann
Gene Kemp
Penelope Lively
Jan Mark
Michael Morpurgo
Ann Pilling
Catherine Sefton

Book series suitable for young fluent readers

Banana Books, published by Heinemann.
Blackbirds, published by Julia MacRae.
Blackie Bears, published by Blackie.
Cartwheels, published by Hamish Hamilton.
Cascades, published by Harper-Collins.
Gazelle, published by Hamish Hamilton.
New Windmill, published by Heinemann.
Pied Piper, published by Methuen.
Read Alone, published by Viking.
Sports Fiction, published by Blackie.
Storybooks, published by Puffin.
Superchamps, published by Heinemann.
Thriller Firsts, published by Blackie.

Picture books for juniors

Ambrus, Victor *Dracula's Bedtime Storybook*, OUP, 1981.
Base, Graeme *Animalia*, Macmillan, 1986.
Briggs, Raymond *Gentleman Jim*, Hamish Hamilton, 1980.
Dolby, Karen *Book of Puzzle Adventures*, Usborne, 1989.
Fc_eman, Michael *War and Peas*, Puffin, 1978.
Handford, Martin *Where's Wally?*, Walker Books, 1987.
Hastings, Selina *Sir Gawain and the Loathly Lady*, Walker Books, 1987.
McAfee, Annalena *The Visitors who Came to Stay*, Hamish Hamilton, 1984.
Oakley, Graham *The Diary of a Church Mouse*, Macmillan, 1989.
Waddell, Martin *Little Dracula's First Bite*, Walker Books, 1990.

What can they read after Blyton?

A list of titles for those children who find it difficult to choose after they have read many titles by one particular author.
Asimov, Isaac *Space Ranger*, Lightning, 1988.
Byars, Betsy *Cracker Jackson*, Puffin, 1986.
Cross, Gillian *Swimathon!* Methuen, 1986.
Howe, James and Deborah *Bunnicula*, Young Lions, 1988.
Leeson, Robert *Wheel of Danger*, Collins, 1986.
Limb, Sue *China Lee*, Lions, 1989.
McBratney, Sam *Zesty*, Hamish Hamilton, 1984.
Mahy, Margaret *Clancy's Cabin*, Puffin, 1987.
Thomas, Ruth *The Runaways*, Beaver, 1988.
Townson, Hazel *Danny, Don't Jump*, Beaver, 1987.
Paton Walsh, Jill *Shine*, Macdonald, 1988.

ACTIVITIES

1. Collaborative writing

Age range
Seven to twelve.

Group size
Two to three children.

What you need
Copies of wordless picture books. (If these are difficult to find in sufficient quantity then choose picture books with just a single line of text below the picture and cover it using strips of card and Blu-Tack.)

What to do
Arrange the children into appropriate groups and tell them to work together to write a text to go with the pictures in the book. Remind them that the text need not be lengthy but it must connect with the illustrations *and* form logical continuous prose from page to page.

When the groups have written the text, ask them to share these versions with other groups, then compare the new text with the original.

Guide the children to consider not only the different perspectives they may have given to the illustrations but also to compare the language used. For example, 'The original version told the events in rhyme and we did not.'

The comparisons will prove very interesting and pupils may genuinely prefer their own version.

2. Text shuffle

Age range
Seven to twelve.

Group size
Three to six children.

What you need
Typed script of a short story, adhesive, scissors, cardboard.

What to do
Stick the copy of the story on to card. Cut up the text into logical divisions based on meaning – this may be in paragraphs or just long sentences, but do not break sentences midway. Give each child in the group a segment, then ask the group to negotiate the order of the text.

You may find it best to start the procedure by asking questions such as, 'Who thinks that they have the first part? Why?' It can be very useful to record the ensuing conversation as the opinions children have about the positioning of their piece of text can be very informative about their knowledge of language. For example, children start using expressions like 'opening lines', 'conclusions', 'development of plot' and so on.

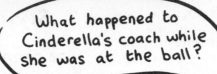

What happened to Cinderella's coach while she was at the ball?

3. Character details

Age range
Seven to twelve.

Group size
Pairs.

What you need
Copies of photocopiable page 155, pens.

What to do
Provide the children with copies of photocopiable page 155. Ask them to think of a particular fictional character (for example, a nursery rhyme character, a fairy tale character, Willy Wonka, etc) and to fill in the details from their chosen character's point of view. By answering the questionnaire the children have to recall the relevant stories and then think up suitable answers for each character, for example:
Name: Snow White.
Alias: Mirror Image.
Age: 17 (always).
Address: Hiho Cottage, Dwarfsville.
Major goal in life: To tell good fruit from bad.
  Encourage the children to pass round their filled in sheets and let the others guess the reason why certain details were chosen. Tasks like this require the children to extract knowledge from their reading and apply it to other circumstances.

4. Extended dialogue

Age range
Seven to twelve.

Group size
Four to six children.

What you need
Tape recorder, paper, pencils, one book per group.

What to do
After a group of children have read a book together ask them to make up extra dialogue or text (written or recorded) tackling issues that do not come into the original story. Introduce the activity by devising questions, such as, 'What did Grandma say when she emerged unhurt from inside the wolf?' or 'How did Jack and his mother dispose of the Giant's body?' Once the children are familiar with the technique, encourage them to devise questions for one another.
  This activity can raise all sorts of issues about what readers are *not* told in stories. The groups may care to speculate reasons for this. This activity should also help the children in structuring their own stories.

5. Cloze

Age range
Seven to twelve.

Group size
Pairs.

What you need
An assortment of texts including poems and stories, a photocopier.

What to do
Photocopies of passages of text or poems with occasional words deleted.
  Hand out the texts and ask the pairs to decide how to fill the gaps. Encourage the children to provide missing words that are not only semantically correct but are also the *best* words in the context. This can introduce children to authorial style and a sense of appropriate language for a context.

Further activity

Instead of randomly deleting words from the passage, delete specific types of word such as all the adjectives or all the adverbs. This will draw the children's attention to how the author has used these parts of speech. It will also help children develop a greater understanding of the use of different parts of speech in their own writing.

6. Word-a-day

Age range
Seven to twelve.

Group size
Whole class.

What you need
Whiteboard, pen.

What to do
Each day write a different word on the board where it can be seen by all the children. Choose words which are interesting, perhaps because they are slightly unusual or perhaps because they are onomatopoeic.

At some time each day draw attention to the word and either explain its meaning, or perhaps explain its derivation. On occasion it might be appropriate to draw parallels between the word for the day and other words connected either by meaning or appearance, for example, kindergarten and 'Kinder-Surprise' (*kinder* is the German word for children).

The object behind this activity is to create an interest in words both for their meaning and the sound they make. It will help both children's vocabulary and their interest in language.

If finding a word-a-day proves too time-consuming then have a 'Word for the week'.

Occasionally, choose a word which is at the root of many other words in English, for example, sign/signature/signal/significance. This attention to patterns within words should help with children's spelling, although the object of the activity is not to provide just another spelling list.

7. Style copy

Age range
Seven to twelve.

Group size
Pairs.

What you need
A variety of picture books, paper, pencils.

What to do
Give each pair of children a picture book and ask them to write their own stories, copying the 'pattern' of the text. For example, if the text is built upon a cumulative pattern, as in, Eric Carle's *The Very Hungry Caterpillar* (Hamish Hamilton, 1970), then the children should copy that style.

Title	Style
My Cat Flossie by Ruth Brown, Beaver Books.	Irony
Grandma Goes Shopping by Ronda and David Armitage, Puffin.	Alliteration
Where's Julius? by John Burningham, Cape.	Grammar
My Brown Bear Barney by D. Butler, Hodder & Stoughton.	Noun phrases
The Wind Blew by Pat Hutchins, Puffin.	Rhyme
Come Away From the Water, Shirley by John Burningham, Picture Lions.	Inferential meaning
If You Give a Mouse a Cookie by Laura Joffe Numeroff, Knight Books.	Circular story
Dr Xargle's Book of Earth Hounds by Jeanne Willis, Andersen Press.	Puns and irony
Stanley Bagshaw and the Fourteen Foot Wheel by Bob Wilson, Puffin.	Parody

Figure 1

Figure 1 suggests appropriate titles and style patterns which the children could copy.

8. Author of the month

Age range
Seven to twelve.

Group size
Whole class.

What you need
Collections of books by one author, tape recorders or pencils and paper.

What to do
Collect together as many copies of as many titles by an author as possible. Use this author as a focus for reading/writing/poetry for a month.

Read aloud sections of the author's works to introduce her to the class and allow time for the children to share responses to the text. These responses may be recorded on to tape for others to listen to, or may be written in the form of a book review.

Try to find out something about the background of the author. (*Books for Keeps* – a magazine about children's books is very useful in this regard.)

At the end of the month arrange activities, such as an author quiz (devised by the children) or a drama session acting out favourite parts of stories by the author.

There is a list of authors you may wish to refer to at the end of this chapter.

CHAPTER 4

Reading non-fiction

In November 1988 the English Working Party led by Professor Brian Cox submitted to the Secretary of State for Education a consultation document outlining the proposals for English in the National Curriculum. This report (English 5–11) proposed dividing AT2, reading into two separate attainment targets:
• the development of the ability to read, understand and respond to all types of writing;
• the development of reading and information-retrieval strategies for the purposes of study.

At the consultation stage many groups, including practising teachers, responded to the National Curriculum Council saying that such a division of reading into separate skills was unnatural and unworkable in the classroom. As a result of this lobbying, the Statutory Orders now only lists one attainment target for reading. However, a closer examination of the wording reveals that all that has

happened is that the two attainment targets have been subsumed into one. The attainment target now reads:
• the development of the ability of read, understand and respond to all types of writing, as well as the development of information-retrieval strategies for the purposes of study (HMSO, 1990).

BACKGROUND

Within English in the National Curriculum there is equal weighting between the reading of all types of writing and reading specifically for study purposes. Traditionally, the primary years are used to concentrate upon the teaching of reading for pleasure and entertainment, leaving the aspects of information-retrieval to secondary school teachers. Under the Statutory Orders this is now no longer possible.

If teachers are to introduce non-fiction reading successfully in the primary years then this needs to be addressed through two crucial areas:
• teaching methods;
• resources.

Teaching methods

Early reading skills are taught through fiction: teachers support developing readers by providing a wide range of fiction for children to read, as well as reading aloud to them, providing constant models of how fiction is read and how it is written. In the past, non-fiction reading hasn't received similar support. However, a child who has learned to read fiction does not automatically become a successful reader of non-fiction.

The different approaches to fiction and non-fiction

• Fast fluent reading is a good style for fiction, whereas with non-fiction it is often better to slow the reading rate to allow the facts to be absorbed.
• Fiction reading is necessarily from the beginning of the book (story) to the end. Non-fiction reading, however, often requires the isolation of a certain passage from a chapter.
• Fiction writing styles seek to engage the interest of the reader throughout the book. In this way an author of fiction builds up a relationship with a reader. The authorial voice is enticing and attractive.

Non-fiction is usually read in brief bursts, and far from having a relationship with the reader, non-fiction texts often seek to preserve the anonymity of the author. The authorial voice is remote and restrained.
• Fiction readers can 'go in cold' – there is no need to know anything about the plot or the characters before reading the book.

When reading non-fiction, however, it is more usual to bring a certain knowledge to the text, with the specific aim of extracting further knowledge from it.

• The vocabulary of fiction can usually be gleaned from the context, while the vocabulary of non-fiction is often unfamiliar and readers may have to acquire new terminology which needs to be cross-referenced within the book.

• All fiction books have a similar format, for example, the text is presented in chapters.

Non-fiction books come in a variety of formats to which the reader needs introducing. Some contain contents and index pages; some have glossaries, notes, bibliographies and so on.

• The language of fiction books has an immediacy which should appeal to a reader. If the style does not attract the reader it is usually sufficient reason to abandon the book and choose something else.

The language of non-fiction usually seeks to present the facts unadulterated by personal opinion.

• Fiction is usually written in the past tense. Non-fiction uses the present tense to express generality. It also uses the definite article to represent universality, for example, 'The ladybird is a small flying beetle.' It is not uncommon for children to ask, 'Which ladybird?'

• Young fiction is illustrated by pictures. However, as children become more fluent readers, they expect to encounter fewer illustrations. Many readers at Key Stage 2 will not pay much attention to the intermittent line drawings in story books, and they do not need to do so in order to understand the story.

Non-fiction is illustrated by diagrams, charts, maps and photographs. Often the text is an explanation of a diagram and the illustrations need careful examination.

• The majority of fiction books are chosen by individual preference.

Non-fiction books are often read because the teacher has directed the child to do so for a particular purpose.

The language of non-fiction books

Non-fiction books are written in a very different style from fiction and these differences can cause the young reader dissatisfaction when reading for information. It is important to be aware of such difficulties facing children in order to help them become familiar with this style.

Non-fiction typically contains:

• Use of abstract words – 'Where the desert met the cultivated land of the valley,

the Valley Temple was built.'
• Use of concealed negatives – 'Also, without a mane, they are less easily seen and can wrestle better in close combat.'
• Use of ellipsis – 'Not only did it bring much-needed water but also a new layer of rich soil that was left on the fields after the flood dried up.'
• Unfamiliar linkage words, such as moreover..., nevertheless... and similarly....
• Complex sentences – 'However, in the north of their range tigers live in snow-covered pine forests, and in the south they live in hot jungles.'
(Quotations from *Pyramids* by Anne Millard, Franklin Watts, 1989, and *Lions and Tigers* by Lionel Bender, Franklin Watts, 1988.)

The language of information books has always been like this and, because it conforms to certain academically agreed conventions, it is likely to remain so. It is up to us to help children become effective processors of this language.

There may be many differences between reading fiction and non-fiction, but it is not impossible to acquaint the children with the various reading skills they will need to become effective readers of non-fiction.

Read-aloud non-fiction

Occasionally, instead of reading fiction to the class, read a non-fiction book. It is difficult to find non-fiction titles which are suitable for reading aloud – those which depend heavily upon illustrations and diagrams are obviously unsuitable. However, there are others with a format closer to a continuous narrative and these can make very successful read-alouds, for example:
The Zoo in the Garden, David Taylor and Mike Birkhead, Boxtree, 1987.
Life Story series, Michael

Chinery, Eagle Books.
Spacewatch series, Michael Chinery, Eagle Books.
Animal Assassins, David Taylor, Boxtree, 1987.

By reading such books aloud you can provide a role model for the features of non-fiction reading, including using a slower pace of delivery and occasionally digressing from the text to relate the information to knowledge that the children already have on the subject (for example, 'I hadn't realised that there are nine spot ladybirds. I had thought that there were only two spot and seven spot.').

When the book has been read, you could refer the children to other books on the same subject that they might like to read.

Toys you can sew

BALLET

All in a Doctor's Day

Ecology

Anima

ce

POND CREATURES

Fashion

Gyn

Group work

Show the children the mechanics of finding information in a non-fiction book. Explain the purpose of the contents, index, glossary, headwords, and so on. Explain the reason behind, for example, sub-headings and bold type, and encourage the children to familiarise themselves with the various layouts of non-fiction books.

You can also use big book versions of information texts to demonstrate the reflective read required to absorb information. When using a big book with a group of children, you can frequently interrupt the reading to recap upon the information extracted. This demonstrates the need to tackle these texts at quite a slow pace, and the constant need to reinterpret and digest what has just been read.

Often we use information texts to ascertain facts quickly. To do this effectively we need to be able to skim through a book (with the aid of the contents or index) and then scan the relevant pages. Children need to be introduced to this method of reading as it does not come naturally to a child used to reading only fiction.

Resources

Non-fiction material dates very quickly and is usually expensive to replace, but it is not really very useful to have shelves filled with inaccurate reference material. You also need to consider stocking books which may be outside the demands of National Curriculum Key Stage 2. Sharks and computer games may not be on the National Curriculum agenda, but many children are interested in these subjects.

Gender differences in reading choice

It is not unusual to discover that boys read more non-fiction than girls. This is reflected in adult reading habits, and it is of some significance as information reading fills a major part of secondary school reading experiences across the curriculum, whereas fiction is confined to English lessons. It is very important that girls are introduced to non-fiction in the primary school so that they are not disadvantaged in the secondary school.

While it would be naive to assume that boys and girls necessarily have different interests in non-fiction topics, it seems reasonable to judge that there will be some differences of interest and these should be reflected in the non-fiction library stock. Are there books on, for example, ecology, medicine, the caring professions, animals, gymnastics, dance and fashion?

It is essential for teachers to help all children become confident readers of both fiction and non-fiction. If children are not supported in selecting and reading non-fiction, even the apparently fluent reader may become discouraged.

ACTIVITIES

1. Alphabet order

Age range
Seven to twelve.

Group size
Five to ten children.

What you need
A variety of information books.

What to do
The purpose of this activity is to encourage children to use their knowledge of alphabet order to access information quickly from non-fiction books.

Ask the children to choose a book then set them the following tasks:
• Find the first entry in the index under the letter 's'. Of course, each child will have a different answer depending on the book that they are using. Take advantage of this by getting the children to cross-reference the information they have found. For example, 'Whose entry under 's' comes first alphabetically?'
• Find out two facts from their information books.
• Find the last entry under the letter 'm'.
These activities give children the experience of handling non-fiction books for reference purposes.

2. Become an expert

Age range
Seven to twelve.

Group size
Six to eight children.

What you need
Sufficient reference books for the group to gather a reasonable amount of information on a chosen subject, tape recorders, paper, pencils, felt-tipped pens.

What to do
Ask the children to choose a subject then to gather as much knowledge about it as possible. It is best to give the group a fairly limited topic to work on,

such as 'The wives of Henry VIII' rather than 'The Tudor Period'.

Give the children advice about recording any information they consider important. For example, they could read a relevant passage on to tape; they could draw pictures based on the text they have read; they could make brief notes; they could group-read a passage and then discuss it. At all costs, discourage children from copying chunks of text from the books.

When the children feel they have a command of their specific topic, ask them to present themselves as a panel of 'experts' to which other members of the class can direct questions. As far as possible, the panel should be encouraged to answer the questions without referring to their notes, but allow them to confer with one another. Explain that if they are asked a question on an aspect outside the range of their study, they are quite entitled to say so to the questioner. If the question is valid but the panel cannot answer it, let them make a note of it and check up the answer at a later date.

The children will need practice with this skill but it will provide them with an incentive to acquire new knowledge. It will also help the rest of the class become more familiar with good questioning techniques.

3. From diagram to prose

Age range
Nine to twelve.

Group size
Whole class.

What you need
A non-fiction book, whiteboard, coloured pens.

What to do
Choose a passage from the book and read it to the class. Ask the children for their responses. These will include both factual recall and incidental comment, perhaps informed by prior reading or knowledge. Jot down on the whiteboard all the contributions from the class in whatever order they are offered. Then ask the children if there is any logical way in which to group the items.

They may suggest grouping the items according to

chronological order, or starting from the most dramatic bit. Indicate on the board which bits of information are related by marking them with the same symbol or colour, then discuss the order in which the groups of facts should be placed.

Remember, there may be no obvious ordering of the facts. Many non-fiction books have an arbitrary order. For example, in a book about Sweden an author might decide to begin with a brief overview of Swedish history and then explain Sweden's geography. However, it would be perfectly acceptable to start with a view of Sweden today and then move into the history, geography, and so on.

Once the children have decided which facts go together, discuss the best way to present those facts. Some information is best conveyed in an illustration; some is better shown in a diagram; other information is best

communicated in prose. Decide together which style best suits which facts and divide the class into groups to present the information on each aspect for the benefit of the other groups.

4. The unanswered questions

Age range
Seven to twelve.

Group size
Four children.

What you need
Several books on each of your chosen topics, paper, pencils.

What to do
Allocate a topic to each group and ask the children to jot

down any question related to the topic to which they have ever wanted to know the answer. For example, if the selected topic is 'Slow-worms', the children might want to know how big they are, or where they live, or what colour they are.

Once they have jotted down their questions, hand out the topic-related books and ask the children to answer as many questions as they can with the aid of the books. This activity gives you ample opportunity to observe which referencing skills have been mastered by which children.

Some children will simply flick through the books at random, hoping to find a relevant piece of text. Other children will remember skills practised earlier and refer to the contents or index. What the children will discover is that not all questions are answered by all books, and indeed some questions are not answered by any of the books, while some questions may not have been very good questions in the first place ('What do slow-worms taste like?'). Some children may like to go away with an unanswered question to try to find the answer elsewhere.

This activity should improve questioning and referencing skills.

5. Making a chart

Age range
Eight to twelve.

Group size
Three children.

What you need
An information book, paper, pencils.

What to do
Choose a page or section from an information book and ask the children to read it and talk about it in their groups. Then ask them to think how this same information could be tabulated into a chart under separate headings. Help the children to decide on the headings of the categories. For example, a piece of writing about polar bears might be divided into columns under the headings:
• Habitat;
• Size;
• Diet;
• Care of young.

Ask the children to enter the facts under the headings in note form. Encourage them to prioritise information, as they will find that not all of it can be fitted into this style of presentation.

Further activity
After selecting and grouping the information under headings, ask the children to write a piece of continuous prose using the chart. This is a particularly good way of discouraging children from copying directly from the book.

6. Copy the style

Age range
Nine to twelve.

Group size
Four children.

What you need
Examples of different kinds of non-fiction books (eg. dictionaries, encyclopaedias, amazing fact books, question and answer books, descriptive information books, life cycle books, etc), paper, pencils.

What to do
Talk to the children about the different ways in which information can be given in non-fiction books and discuss with them which format would be most suitable for their own piece of information writing. (It is a good idea to base this activity around a topic that the class are exploring at the time.) Ask the children to write the information in the style they feel is most appropriate for their aspect of the topic.

These writing tasks need not be lengthy. It is better that the children learn to present information in particular ways rather than feel that absolutely everything must be written down. Many of the styles of presentation would be best explored with lots of groups using the same format, perhaps to compile an encyclopaedia.

7. Getting to grips with a glossary

Age range
Nine to twelve.

Group size
Pairs.

What you need
Glossaries from books related to a topic which the children have studied.

What to do
When the class is near the end of a particular study provide pairs of children with copies of a glossary with the headwords deleted. Ask the children to discover what the missing headwords might be.

Some of these will be obvious from the definitions given in the glossary; others will only become apparent if the children check back through the book. This activity not only encourages good reflection on a topic which has been studied, but it also gives children further practice at finding their way around non-fiction books and using alphabetical order in a systematic way.

CHAPTER 5

Reading poetry

'At its best, poetry helps children to become vigorous and adventurous and graceful users of words, nourishes the elusive substance of the human imagination and shows them how to think well.' (Jack Ousbey, 1988)

Many teachers feel that poetry requires special attention. The truth is that it requires the same degree of careful attention as the rest of the reading curriculum. Understandably, teachers want to offer children good and worthwhile experiences, but they frequently express doubts about how to bring children and poetry together. Questions such as, 'What poetry should I read to my class?', 'How often should I read poetry to the class?' and 'What should be the outcome of the children's encounters with poetry?' are often asked. Many of the questions reflect uncertainties about the teacher's own abilities to read and appreciate poetry. Whatever the reasons for these uncertainties, Jack Ousbey's suggestion that exposure to poetry is the way in which children will come to understand the power of language and appreciate the relationship between thoughts and words, applies equally to any reader of poetry.

BACKGROUND

In order to help children turn readily to poetry, it is important that it is an integral part of the reading curriculum. Hearing and reading poetry provides the listener or reader with experiences similar to those offered by other forms of literature. For example, it can give pleasure, explain situations, events or phenomena and satisfy emotional or intellectual needs. What distinguishes it from other literature is the way in which poetry achieves its effects. Rhyme, rhythm, metaphor and text layout are features particular to poetry and contribute to its effectiveness. Exposure to a wide range of poetry will encourage children to become committed readers of poetry, with an ear for language and a feel for its tune.

Above all, children need to hear poetry spoken and read aloud. Ted Hughes (1963) summed up the power of poetry like this:

'What matters most, since we are listening to poetry and not to prose, is that we hear the song and dance in the words. The dance and the song engage the deepest roots of our minds and carry the poet's words down into our depths. And the final sway that the poet has over our minds is largely the hidden waves of song and the motion of the dance in phrasing of the words that it compels us to share as we read or hear it.'

The teacher's role

As the teacher, it is up to you to provide ample time, material and opportunity for all the children in your class to hear and read as wide a range of poetry as possible. Inevitably, planning and resourcing the 'poetry curriculum' raises questions of time, quantity and material. Whatever decisions are made, it is important that poetry is always an integral part of classroom reading. It should never be considered as something to be 'done' and then forgotten about until next term. The question of how many poems should be offered in a year is not easy to answer. It has been suggested that teachers should aim to present between 60 and 100 poems during the course of a school year – and that these should be read on at least two occasions.

Whenever the moon and stars are set,
Whenever the wind is high,
All night long in the dark and wet,
A man goes riding by.

Look Michael, here are some more poems by Janet and Allan Ahlberg!

Sport Stories

Finding and selecting poems

When selecting material, consider the differences between and the interests of individual children. Your initial selection of poems may not be to your taste, but by encouraging children to start with poems they like, you can then extend their range of choice. Naturally you will want to introduce poetry that you feel offers new opportunities, but this is not easy to do if you ignore the children's interests.

It is very tempting to select poems according to the current classroom topic or theme, or poems that are short and do not require a great deal of time to be spent on reading them. Of course, there is a place for this, but they should not become the sole reasons for selecting poems. Your ultimate aim is to offer as wide a range of poetry as possible to all the children in the class, a range which reflects the richness and diversity of both language and poetry.

Don't forget to include both anthologies and 'individual author' volumes. It may be that by browsing through an anthology the child picks out a poem of particular appeal. If the school collection also has many volumes of poetry by single authors, then children can begin to talk about favourite poets just as they do about favourite authors. Anthologies can introduce poets to readers or remind them of favourite or half-remembered poems. A collection of one poet's work allows an introduction to be taken further, and children also come to know and recognise the writing of different poets.

Selection criteria should include consideration of the following points.

Language and form
• Is the language memorable?
• Does it invite repetition and/or reflection?
• What form is used? Does the poem rhyme? Is the verse regular or free? How is rhythm used?

Breadth and balance
• What is the mood of the poem? Are a range of moods and emotions included in the classroom selection (serious, comic, nonsense, reflective)?
• Is the classroom selection balanced? Does it contain a range of types of poetry (narrative poems, limericks, ballads)?

They live on crispy pancakes
Of yellow tide-foam

Complexity

• Does the poem provide opportunities for exploration or reflection?
• Does the poem have unlimited 'shelf life'? Does it warrant rereading so that, over time, meaning can be reconsidered, reshaped or better understood?

If selection takes account of the above criteria, children will have access to a range of poetry that encourages reading and discussion, and promotes interest and pleasure in language.

Introducing and presenting poetry

The children's encounters with poetry ought to be enjoyable. If hearing, sharing and reading poetry are memorable and pleasurable experiences, children will develop a 'poetic memory'. This store of memories will in turn enrich their reflections, discussions and writing. The Kingman Report (1988) said, 'As children read more, discuss what they have read and move through the range of writing in English, they amass a store of images from half-remembered poems, of lines from plays, of phrases, rhythms and ideas. Such a reception of language allows the individual greater possibilities of production of language.'

Helping children experience poetry, rather than 'comprehend' it, is a useful starting point. This does not mean that a poem should not be considered, discussed or analysed, rather that it should not be used for comprehension exercises. And indeed, the images and layers of meaning that are part and parcel of poetry hardly lend themselves to the notion of right and wrong that is implicit in a comprehension exercise.

How then might poetry be introduced? First of all, abandon any idea that hearing or reading poetry should lead to a particular outcome. Poetry can stimulate a variety of responses, including questioning, puzzling over the meaning, repeating memorable words and phrases, drawing or writing. Any response may be public or private. What matters most is that poetry is enjoyed and presented in a variety of ways.

Poetry and knowledge about language

Encouraging children to think about how they respond to a particular poem, and why, helps them to develop their knowledge about language. Poetry achieves its effects through particular arrangements and juxtapositions of words, phrases, lines, verses and ideas. It distils language, can make the usual unusual and encapsulate thoughts, feelings and actions. When we hear or read poetry, we respond according to our experience of the world, of other reading, and of words and their meanings. If children are encouraged to think about their initial response and helped to discuss how a poem affected them, they can then focus on how this was achieved. In this way they can be helped to understand the ways in which language can trigger or manipulate response.

Asking the group to identify words and phrases that produce particular effects and discussing the way in which these are accomplished, can develop an awareness of the power of language. For example, they are helped to realise the effectiveness of literary devices such as rhyme, repetition, simile and metaphor. They are also helped to appreciate the purposes and use of sound patterns and rhythms. Discussions based on reflection and response draw on what the reader or listener knows. Helping children to make this knowledge explicit deepens their existing understanding in a meaningful context.

Poetry in the classroom

Reading aloud to the class

This allows the teacher to introduce new poems and to reread old favourites. A read-aloud session provides opportunities for just listening, joining in or discussion. It is also a time when the children can hear and feel the power and rhythm of language. Asking the children to comment on what they have heard will elicit a wide range of

I really like Michael Rosen because he makes me laugh but also because he's really clever!

responses and help them appreciate that these may differ but are all valid.

Possible questions might be, 'What did you think of that?' or 'Did any particular part of the poem appeal to you?' Encouraging the children to reflect on the whole poem allows them to consider such things as gist, use of language and favourite phrases. It is only when they have responded to the whole poem that they can consider specific details.

Reading poetry to the class allows even the least confident readers to hear and enjoy texts that they could not read independently. Reading and rereading poetry helps you to find out children's preferences and to extend their knowledge of poetry. Frequently a poem that has been read to the class becomes a favourite and the children become very keen to read it for themselves.

Class reading or browsing

Set aside a regular time when children can read poetry for themselves. This could be part of the time allocated to silent reading. Explain that during this particular session you would like the children to look through, sample and read a selection of poetry. The choice should be left to them, but it means that the class book collection needs to provide ample selection.

Time spent in this way allows the children to discover poems that they like, read old favourites or reread a poem that has been introduced during a read-aloud session. It also provides time for quiet reflection and reconsideration.

This quiet reading time could be followed up by asking for volunteers to read a poem that they particularly liked to the rest of the class. However, nothing specific need result from the session and the experience of sampling and savouring poetry can be left as a private one.

Group reading

• Ask groups to select poems on a theme, or by a particular poet. Each group could present their choice to the rest of the class or in assembly. Suggest to the children that they should be prepared to say why they chose a particular poem or poet. Explain that saying, 'I like it' is not sufficient reason for the selection. They need to reflect on what they liked about it. Was it the words? Was it the idea? Have they been in a similar situation or did it remind them of anything else?

• Choral reading. Although this sounds like a dated activity, it has great value in the poetry curriculum. By encouraging all the children to partake in this, even those who find reading poetry difficult can experience its rhythm and power. The support of the group often helps less confident children to learn the words, which in turn helps them to read this and other poems. Initially a short four-line verse may be the best choice, but as children become more familiar with this they can tackle longer, more demanding poems. For example, members of the group could each be responsible for one verse or one voice as it occurs in the poem.

• Poetry can also be used with groups for discussion. Give each member of the group a

Tiger, tiger burning bright
In the forests of the night

Far and few, far and few
Are the lands where the
jumblies live

copy of the poem and suggest that they read it to each other. Discussion might arise naturally but it can be helpful to have a set of questions around which the children can focus their discussion. What is this poem about? Was the poem to do with feelings, people, ideas or anything else? Do you think the poem would have been better as a story? Which particular words or phrases do you think are the most interesting? Is any line repeated? Do you think this a good idea?

Alternatively, some questions could be related to the specific poems and put into an envelope stuck in the back of the book.

However, there are children for whom this is an impossible task. They can be helped by being included in choral group work where their peers support their efforts, but do not single them out for a public performance unless they volunteer.

Learning poetry by heart

To force children to learn by heart may destroy the love of poetry we are hoping to create; however, encouraging children to repeat poems either in their entirety or in part will give them a power of recall which will remain with them for life. This recall is both potent and valuable. Initially this can be a supported activity, with the teacher reading and rereading a favourite poem and encouraging the children to join in. Many of the children will discover that they have learned the poem by heart.

Suggested poetry titles

When I Dance James Berry, (Hamish Hamilton, 1988).
Please Mrs. Butler Allan Ahlberg, illus. Fritz Wegner (Viking Kestrel, 1985).
Come on into My Tropical Garden Grace Nichols, illus. Caroline Binch (A & C Black, 1988).
Four O'Clock Friday John Foster (OUP, 1991).
Jack the Treacle Eater Charles Causley, illus. Charles Keeping (Macmillan, 1987).
The Highwayman Alfred Noyes, illus. Charles Keeping (OUP, 1981).

Song of the City Gareth Owen (Fontana, 1985).
Quick, Let's Get Out of Here Michael Rosen, illus. Quentin Blake (Andre Deutsch, 1983).

Anthologies

Ten Golden Years compiled by Chris Powling & Sally Grindley (Walker Books, 1989).
I Saw Esau ed. Iona & Peter Opie, illus. Maurice Sendak (Walker Books, 1992).
Wordspells ed. Judith Nicholls, illus. Alan Baker (Faber, 1988).
The Rattle Bag ed. Seamus Heaney & Ted Hughes (Faber, 1982).
The Kingfisher Book of Comic Verse, ed. Roger McGough, illus. Caroline Holden (Kingfisher, 1988).

ACTIVITIES

1. The wall frieze

Age range
Any age.

Group size
Whole class working in groups of four.

What you need
Copy of a poem or a ballad, materials for making a frieze (paper, paint, adhesive, scrap materials etc).

What to do
Read the poem or ballad to the class. Ask each group to select an episode from it, making sure that they have each chosen a different event. Ask them to identify the relevant verse/verses or part of the poem.

Encourage the groups to plan how they could best represent their chosen event. Let them choose a medium such as painting or collage to depict it.

Display the groups' work chronologically, together with the relevant verse/verses.

2. The poetry display board

Age range
Any age.

Group size
Individuals or pairs.

What you need
Designated wall space, wide selection of poetry books, paper, pencils, felt-tipped pens.

What to do
Ask the children to select a favourite poem, either by theme or author. Let them write out the poem and illustrate it as they choose.

Make a display of the children's work. Review the display regularly so that it stays interesting and alive.

Variations
• Ask the children to select a 'Top Ten' of favourite poetry and make a display as described above.
• Ask the class to vote on the two poems they would like to have with them on a desert island.

3. Hot seating

Age range
Any age.

Group size
Whole class.

What you need
Copies of a dramatic poem or ballad.

What to do
Read the poem with the children, then discuss the various characters and their actions.

Invite the children to volunteer to take on the role of one of the characters. Sit the volunteer in the 'hot seat' and ask the rest of the group to ask her questions about the events in the poem and the part she has played in it. Make clear to the 'character' that she must answer in role.

4. Freeze frame

Age range
Any age.

Group size
Whole class, working in pairs or threes.

What you need
Copies of a dramatic poem or ballad.

What to do
Read the poem with the children. Discuss the characters, actions and events in the poem and the places where these occur. Depending on the event and character, ask

the children to work in twos and threes to represent one of the scenes in the poem in a 'still' image.

Let the groups take turns to present their 'tableaux' and ask the rest of the class to try to identify the part represented.

This can be developed by asking the children in the 'frame' each to say a line in character.

5. Guess my title

Age range
Any age.

Group size
Whole class.

What you need
A selection of short poems, whiteboard, pens.

What to do
Read a short poem to the class, omitting the title, and ask for suggestions for an appropriate title.

Write the children's suggestions on the board and discuss them. Ask questions such as, 'What made you

suggest that title? Was it a word? Was it an idea?'

Finally reveal the poet's choice. Discuss with the children the effect this title has upon their understanding of the poem.

6. Order, order!

Age range
Any age.

Group size
Two to four children.

What you need
Word processor with a large typeface, scissors, card, adhesive.

What to do
Type out a selection of poems, using a large typeface. Mount each poem on to stiff card, then cut it up into separate verses or lines.

Give the groups the pieces of the poems. Ask them to read the texts and discuss a possible order. When they have decided on the most likely order, give the group copies of the original and let them discuss any variations.

This activity helps children appreciate that poetry does not have to rhyme, that it can be linked by word patterns, rhythm or ideas.

7. Class anthology

Age range
Any age.

Group size
Whole class.

What you need
A wide selection of poetry books, paper, pencils, felt-tipped pens, hole punch, ring binder or ribbon.

What to do
At the beginning of the term tell the children that they are going to make an anthology for their book corner. Encourage them to be on the lookout for suitable poems that they think other children might like to hear or read. Make sure that they are regularly hearing a range of poetry.

At intervals, ask the class to nominate poems that they feel should be included in their anthology. Keep a list of these suggestions.

Towards the end of the term ask the children to have an editorial conference to make the final selection. When this is agreed, let the children write out and illustrate the poems as appropriate.

Let them use a ring binder for their anthology or bind it themselves with ribbon. Finally, ensure that the anthology meets standard publishing conventions, for example, include an index of first lines, a list of authors, etc.

8. Meaning detective

Age range
Any age.

Group size
Whole class, working in smaller groups.

What you need
A selection of poems that have unusual dialect or invented words, pencils, paper.

What to do
Give the groups copies of the poems to read. Ask the children to identify any words that they do not recognise and to discuss what they think the words might mean. Ask them to write down their definitions.

Collect their interpretations and display them on the wall alongside a copy of the poem. This is an ideal activity for helping children reflect on and develop their knowledge about language.

CHAPTER 6

Reading the media

'Media education should be concerned not only with modern mass media such as television, cinema and radio, but also with all public forms of communication including printed materials (books as well as newspapers) and computerised sources of information such as data bases.' (English for Ages 5 to 16, 9.7)

BACKGROUND

The above quote from the Cox Report reminds us of the range of printed material, television and film that are part of the everyday world. Helping children to learn how to read all forms of communication is an important part of the reading curriculum. After all, a great deal of the reading that takes place outside school is not from books. We are constantly bombarded with information: newspapers, television news programmes and documentaries tell us about local and world events; films, soap operas and serials tell us stories of other people's lives; advertisements seek to tell us the merits and benefits of a host of products. In order to help children become questioning and critical readers of the whole range of reading matter that they encounter, it is important to reconsider what we understand by 'being a reader'.

Traditionally, and by habit, reading in school has been associated with books. As teachers of reading we are concerned with introducing children to the world of books. Once they can read, we continue to promote reading through the provision of books and may pay little attention to the range of reading that is part of the child's life outside school. Of course, encouraging an interest in books and a love of reading is one of the primary aims of the reading curriculum, but to be fully literate in today's world requires much more than just the ability to read books. In today's society, being literate means being able to read and interpret a vast range of varying visual and written texts and to understand their different messages.

Readers need to be able to interpret different forms of presentation and discuss such things as television and radio programmes, computer displays, magazines, newspapers, pamphlets, brochures and so on. By giving children opportunities to reflect on and discuss the range of non-literary texts that they encounter regularly, we can help expand their understanding of how different media work and develop their knowledge of language.

Did anyone see "Jubilee Road" on telly last night?

Television and reading

Many children see reading as a school activity with little relevance to their life outside. As teachers we have been remiss in not recognising the central role that television can play in developing children as critical readers. Television, a medium with which most children are very familiar, can be a useful springboard for exploring their reactions and responses to what they see and hear.

Watching television is an activity that most families engage in. They may not consciously decide to sit down and watch programmes together, but within the general domestic dialogue and comment that often accompanies viewing, children hear people responding to the 'text on the screen' and come to know that opinion is part of viewing. This experience and knowledge can be used as a starting point for classroom discussion of a book.

Like books, television can and does provide opportunities to experience other worlds, understand particular situations or consider meanings beyond the literal. As children watch stories on television they develop an awareness of character and plot. They learn to reflect on what has been seen and heard and to predict what might happen next. Soap operas, so often scorned as 'junk', can be used as a basis for discussion in the classroom. Children can be helped to think about realism, stereotyping and bias.

Are the characters and settings convincing? Is the plot intended to be realistic? What are the roles of the different groups in the stories? Questions such as these enable children to consider the ways in which different characters perceive the same story event. Also, because soap operas involve many characters and approach story telling by 'sampling' many different stories, they can be used to help children appreciate 'stories within stories'. Children learn that even though the viewer or reader may be being presented with one event, other events are occurring simultaneously.

By encouraging critical discussion of television story and drama, we can help children to realise that, as viewers, they 'read' and respond to texts, and that they can be made to take a certain point of view by the way the 'facts' have been presented, for example to feel sympathy with the actions of a character. So, in many ways, learning to read television can complement and enhance the more literary reading that takes place in school. Don't forget, reading is frequently encouraged by the serialisations of children's books that are shown on television. The increased interest generated by the dramatisation of a story can be one of the most effective ways of leading the children to sample other works by the same author.

The radio and reading

The use of the radio in schools may be less popular these days than the television but it, too, can provide a forum for discussion. Children need to be aware of the ways in which voices, music and other sound effects can create images.

Listening to plays to show how characters are created by the way in which they speak can help children become more aware of stereotyping. It is possible to tape a variety of different plays and use them to compare how the producers have created the impressions of the various characters. For example, do the villains speak with a particular kind of voice or accent? How do the listeners know which are the heroes and heroines? How are the elderly portrayed? How are men and women portrayed? What effect does music produce on the listener and why is it used in particular places?

Children need to learn how to 'read' the radio in the same way as they need to become critical readers of the television.

Reading and advertising

Advertisements are ideal for helping children to come to understand author intention. By examining the language of advertisements they can discover how it can be used to manipulate the reader. By looking at language in this way, children can become aware of the power of the catch-phrase and how it may affect the reader. Some advertisements rely on their reader having a background of knowledge which will deepen the ultimate effect, for example, the lager advertisement which exploits the Arthurian myth.

Word processing and reading

Most children these days have access to a word processor at school. Whatever time is available, word processor use should be well spent, giving the children worthwhile experiences. Access to a word processor means that not only is it possible for children to produce printed work but also that it can be published for others to read.

This purposeful use of technology encourages both reading and writing. The writer becomes the reader as he constantly rereads and refines what has been written. Involvement in the process of drafting, editing and publishing helps children understand the reader's needs and how the presentation of texts can influence reading. For instance, producing a newspaper, an advertisement or a set of instructions all require very different knowledge and use of language. Learning how to create such texts develops children's knowledge about language and at the same time gives them greater ability to read them.

Reading and the computer

There are a considerable number of computer programs available which require children to read a variety of texts. The following are a brief selection of those that teachers have found to be especially useful. Further details can be found in Resources, page 192.

'Developing Tray'
This program enables children to recreate a hidden text that the teacher has previously selected. The teacher types the text on to the program and the children attempt to discover it through a process of trial and error. The children have to predict and speculate on likely words, phrases and letter combinations and put them on to the screen. This program has been highly successful for many years.

'Dinosaur Discovery'
The players have to read entries in a log book in order to solve the problems that they encounter.

'Front Page Extra'
This program enables children to produce their own newspaper and, through this, they come to appreciate the layout and the style of writing used in newspapers.

'News Bulletin'
This program provides children with the opportunity to create and read teletexts.

ACTIVITIES

1. And now the news – 1

Age range
Any age.

Group size
Whole class.

What you need
A video recording of a news event, pens, whiteboard.

What to do
Show the whole class the news clip. Discuss with them what was shown and what was said. (You may have to show the clip several times to help the children think about and separate the images and the words.)

Ask the children to decide which two or three shots were the most memorable and list them on the board. Then ask them to identify which words accompanied which picture. List the appropriate words against each picture. Use the list to discuss why those images and words were used, and whether the information given was relevant to the news item. Were both facts and opinion included and, if so, why?

2. And now the news – 2

Age range
Any age.

Group size
Two to four children.

What you need
A range of newspaper reports of the same event, paper, pencils.

What to do
Give each group a newspaper report. Ask the children to read their cuttings and to decide what are the main points in the report. If there are any pictures, what information do they give?

Let each group make a list of the points from their news item, including any they have found in the pictures.

When the groups have finished, ask a representative from each to report their

findings to the whole class. Use these as a basis for further discussion. Do all the newspapers report the same facts? If there are differences, why might this be? What kind of language is used to report the event? Why do newspapers use a particular type of language? Do all newspapers use the same kind of language? What do the children think of the varying reports? Can they suggest any reasons for any differences or discrepancies they have found?

Further activity
Use this activity as a point for a discussion about the ways in which different media present the same news.

3. Reading along

Age range
Any age.

Group size
Whole class.

What you need
A video recording of a dramatisation of a children's book, a copy of the book.

What to do
Choose some episodes from the book to read to the children. Ask them how they imagine the characters look, what they wore, how they spoke and to describe the setting of the action.

Show them the parallel episodes from the video version. Ask them to think about the way the story is told on film. Has anything been left out or changed? Is a narrator's voice used in any part of the film or is the story told entirely through the characters' actions and dialogue? How much do the scene changes contribute to the story? How do the scenes change in the book?

Encourage the children to suggest reasons for the differences and why different media tell the same story in different ways. Can the book do anything that the film cannot and vice versa? Which do they prefer and why?

4. Advertisement language

Age range
Any age.

Group size
Pairs.

What you need
A selection of advertisements cut from magazines or newspapers. (These could all be for similar products, for something the children would be particularly interested in or a representative selection of current advertisements.)

What to do

Give each pair of children an advertisement and ask them to consider the following questions.

• What impression is the picture trying to give about the product?
• What impression do the words give about the product?
• What information does the advertisement give?
• If there are people in the picture, what are they like? Why are they shown like that?
• Do the words try to make the reader buy the product? If so, which words?
• Does the picture try to make the reader buy the product? If so, how?

When the pairs have had time to discuss these questions, bring the group together to share their findings. Make a list of any words or images that the children have identified as being persuasive. (This list could be displayed as a resource to help them produce an advertisement for a forthcoming class or school event.)

5. Cartoon characters

Age range
Any age.

Group size
Whole class.

What you need
Video recordings of television cartoons, large sheet of paper, pen.

What to do
Show the children one of the cartoons.

Divide the paper into three columns. Ask the children to tell you all the characters that were in the film and list them in the first column. Then ask them what qualities each character had and write these in the appropriate place in the middle column. Finally, ask the children how they knew what the characters were like. For example, was it what they did and/or said? Was it how they said it? Was it what they wore? Write these in the third column.

Use the chart to discuss how character can be suggested and portrayed. This activity is useful in helping children explore and discuss stereotyping.

CHAPTER 7

Group reading

'If three or four persons agree to read the same book, and each brings his own remarks upon it, at some set appointed hour for conversation, and they communicate mutually their sentiments on the subject, and debate about it in a friendly manner, this practice will render the reading of any author more abundantly beneficial to every one of them.' (Watts, 1811.)

BACKGROUND

Why is group reading important?

Historically group reading fell into disrepute because it tended to be a whole-class activity through which the teacher could claim to have heard every child read every day. The children were each given a copy of the 'reading book' and the reading assessment and progress was judged by the few lines that the child read aloud in front of the rest of the form. Many children read other books under the desk while waiting their turn, or read ahead if some of their peers made slow progress. This experience still remains vivid in the memories of those who endured it and explains why group reading has taken so long to come back into classrooms. However, it is increasingly being recognised as an important part of children's reading development for the following reasons.

• It enables the pupils to discuss the text and, through this discussion, to understand the story at a deeper level.

• It encourages children to explore the characters and plot of the book in greater depth.

• It allows children with similar interests to share a read reflecting those interests.

• Teachers can 'hear' children read in a short period of time and consequently have time to discuss the different aspects of the text with them. This is an efficient use of teacher time.

• Teachers can observe children reading aloud in a less threatening situation than in one-to-one practice and often different strengths are revealed.

• It gives a real purpose for children to read aloud with intonation and expression; these skills become increasingly redundant as children become silent readers.

• In talking about a book with others, children acquire the language of book talk. For example, 'I liked the ending...', 'I wonder why the author...?'.

• It is possible for weaker and more reticent readers to be part of a mixed-ability group, and to see and hear how other children read.

• The children enjoy it!

Techniques for successful group reading

What size should the groups be?

This is often dictated by the resources and interests of the pupils. However, most teachers advocate four in an unsupervised group and up to six in a group with an adult. These group sizes seem to ensure that all children participate in any discussion and are more prepared to listen to each other. Larger groups can mean that some children remain 'passengers' or never have the chance to express their views. There is a place for groups of every size, including pairs, but resources must be chosen with care if the group is large. Obviously, reading plays could involve the whole class, but some children could have long waits between their contributions and may become restless and bored.

How should the groups be chosen?

Groups should be chosen in ways that offer many different combinations of children. Initially friendship groups seem to work the best as the children seem more prepared to discuss in this group, but groups could also be selected because of a common interest, or by ability or gender. A group of quiet readers or 'loud' readers can have some interesting results.

Managing the group read

Supervised groups

When the teacher or another adult sits with a group, opportunities arise to explore the book in ways that are rarely possible with an individual child.

For instance, you might ask the group to predict from the title what the book will be about. The group could spend time reading and discussing the cover blurb, talking about the author and other books they have read by the same author, looking at the illustrations and commenting on how much these add to or detract from the book.

Once you begin reading, it is rarely productive to insist that the pupils read round in order, even in a small group. Once the group has become used to group reading they generally like to decide among themselves who should read first, next, and so on. This gives the opportunity for the more reticent reader to select a shorter piece of text while at the same time participating in a longer reading session. You can also demonstrate how to read aloud, possibly by varying the rate of delivery – such as reading slowly an ironic passage, alerting the listener to the double meaning. It is especially valuable to demonstrate reading non-fiction texts which can pose so many problems to young readers (see Chapter 4, 'Reading non-fiction').

Finally, you can orchestrate the discussion that should follow a group read. Once the children have become familiar with this approach they can continue the practice when they are members of unsupervised reading groups.

Unsupervised groups

Children do need to be encouraged to organise themselves. They need to experience the necessary negotiating within a group that allows them to take part and to wait their turn, to listen to others and to be prepared to relinquish a point they want to make because the discussion has moved on beyond it. This may sound an impossible goal, but if children are not given the opportunity to learn then it will remain impossible.

Often spontaneous discussion naturally follows a good story, but it is advisable to have some tasks available if this does not happen (see activities on pages 72 to 74).

How often should group reading take place?

Every child should have the opportunity to take part in a group reading session but whether this takes place once a week or less frequently depends on the resources available and the needs of the group. The likelihood is that as children become accustomed to this activity it will take place more frequently.

What about the disruptive pupil?

There will always be one or two children who find it very difficult settling to a task, especially if it is not directly controlled by the teacher. If the whole class is involved in group work you may decide to separate such pupils from the others. However, it is essential that you discuss the reason for this and invite them to take part as soon as possible; continuous isolation is not a final solution.

If there is a group of disruptive pupils in the class it can be beneficial to place them together and to set them the challenge of producing something to share with the rest of the class at the end of the session. Peer pressure can be very effective and so can success – it is unlikely that this group would want to be seen as the only ones who were unable to present something to the rest of the class.

Sometimes the task itself is part of the problem – maybe it is too difficult, or not demanding enough. It is essential that you select tasks that are within the ability of the group and that all members of the group understand what they have to do.

What resources work well in group reading?

Almost any interesting texts work well in group reading sessions, but to start with it is easier to give the pupils texts that can be read at one go, so short stories, poems and selected pages of non-fiction are ideal. It is also advisable to try to provide texts that the group can read easily. The purpose is not to stretch their reading ability but to allow them the chance to discuss the texts. This is far more likely to occur if the reading is within their range.

Suggested titles for children in Y3-Y4

Ahlberg, J. & A. *The Clothes Horse and Other Stories*, Viking Kestrel, 1987.
Butterworth, C. *My World* series, eg *Beavers*, Macmillan, 1988.
Davies, G.C. *Oranges and Lemons* series, Level 1 and 2, Blackwell.
Gavin, J. *The Magic Orange Tree and Other Stories*, Magnet, 1987.
Holbrook Jackson (ed.), *The Complete Nonsense of Edward Lear*, Faber, 1947.
King-Smith, D. *Tumbleweed*, Gollancz, 1987.
Kipling, R. *The Just So Stories*, Macmillan.
Lord, J.V. *The Giant Jam Sandwich*, Piccolo, 1988.
Mahy, M. *Chocolate Porridge and Other Stories*, Puffin, 1989.

Marshall, J. *Three Up a Tree*, A & C Black, 1986.
Tomlinson, J. *The Otter who Wanted to Know*, Magnet, 1979.
Webb, K. (ed.), *I Like This Poem*, Puffin, 1979.
Wilson, A.N. *Hazel the Guinea Pig*, Walker Books, 1990.
Wright, K. (ed.) *Poems for 9-Year-Olds and Under*, Puffin, 1985.

Suggested titles for children in Y5-Y6

Crossley-Holland, K. *British Folk Tales*, Orchard Books, 1987.
Dickens, C. *A Christmas Carol*, Gollancz, 1989.
Fadiman, C. (ed.) *Puffin Children's Treasury,* Puffin, 1987.
Graham, E. (ed.) *A Puffin Book of Verse*, Puffin, 1969.
Kipling, R. *The Jungle Book*, Macmillan, 1983.
Oakley, G. *The Church Mouse*, Macmillan, 1989.
Smith, D. *The Hundred and One Dalmatians*, Piccolo, 1975.
Ward, P. *The Adventures of Charles Darwin*, CUP, 1986.
Webb, K. (ed.) *I Like This Story*, Puffin, 1986.

Plays for group reading

Junior Drama Workshop
(Ed. Ginny Lapage, Nelson)
These are plays for large groups with the implication that they could be performed by a whole class. Ideas for putting on a production are included.

Playreaders
(Ed. B. Root, Nelson)
These are divided into two levels, for lower and upper juniors. The group sizes vary between eight to twelve readers.

Playmakers
(S. Lane and M. Kemp, CUP)
These are plays for Y4-Y6. Many of the plays are adaptations of famous stories.

Read Around 2
(P. Grokes and N. Grimshaw, Hodder & Stoughton)
These are easy plays for eight- to twelve-year-olds.

Read Around the World 1 and 2
(Jane Moran, Hodder & Stoughton)
These are folk tales selected for small group reading.

Sunshine Plays
(Heinemann)
These plays can be purchased separately from the Sunshine Books. They are for small group reading and relate to levels 6-11 of the Sunshine books.

Take-Part
(S. Lane and M. Kemp, Ward Lock)
These plays are deliberately written for children with a wide range of reading ability. Suggested reading ages for each character are discreetly provided inside the back cover. The plays range from traditional tales to adaptations of classic stories, such as Alice in Wonderland.

Whodunnits
(MGP)
These plays are for small groups and the readers are given clues to the culprit throughout the text. The group is expected to solve the mystery after they have read the play.

Questions to encourage discussion of texts

Although spontaneous discussion can arise after a group has read a text together, it is often necessary to structure the talk along certain paths. The following questions could help, but they do need to be adapted specifically to the chosen texts. However, it is not a good idea to set questions after every group read. Remember, discussion can be valuable even if it only lasts five minutes.

Some teachers write questions or instructions for activities on to cards and keep them in an envelope attached to the inside back cover of the books. Children are then encouraged to select one of these after they have finished their initial discussion.

General questions

Before reading the book
• What do you think this book is about?
• Who wrote it? Have you read any other books by this author?
• Where would you look to get a general idea about this book (eg blurb, contents, index)?
• Who illustrated this book? Do you know any other books illustrated by this artist? Do you like the illustrations? Do they make you want to read the book?

After reading the book
• What part did you like best?
• Did it remind you of any other stories you have read?
• Would this make a good TV programme?
• Who would you give this book to? Someone older than you, your friend, someone younger? Why?
• Would you like to read this book again? If so, on your own or in a group?

Fiction questions

Plot questions
• Did you like the beginning of this book?
• Did you guess the ending?
• Which was the most exciting part?
• Did any part of the story come as a surprise?
• Can you think of a different way to end the story?

Character questions
• Which character would you have liked to be? Why?
• Did you change your opinion of anyone during the story?
• What would you like to ask a character in the book?
• What clues gave you the impression of who was good and who was bad?
• Can you draw an identikit picture of any of the characters?

Non-fiction questions
• How helpful was the contents page?
• Did the glossary help you to understand the vocabulary better?
• Can you tell your group or partner one new piece of information you can remember from the book?
• Show your group the illustration you found the most interesting and say why you chose it.
• Can you think of some questions that were not answered by the book?
• Can you put some of this information into a different form (eg a graph, a diagram, a map)?

ACTIVITIES

1. Character growth chart

Age range
Nine to eleven.

Group size
Small groups (four to six children).

What you need
Story with strong character portrayal (at least one book per two children), copies of photocopiable page 156, pencils.

What to do
Children's understanding of character can be helped by tracking how the author discloses a particular character. Ask the group to read the story, then to choose one of the major characters. For example, they might choose Allan Ahlberg's *Jolly Postman*.

Each member of the group should look through the text to see what characteristics the author mentions and write them down. They should also look at the illustrations to see what characteristics the illustrator has shown and note them down in the same way.

Give the children each a copy of photocopiable page 156 and ask them to write down these impressions in the first column of the sheet. Encourage the group to share these ideas and to check whether they agree and to see if they learn something new. Ask them to write these new impressions in the second column and, if they have changed their opinion, add the reason in column three.

For a more extended activity, let groups of children trace the development of a character through a longer book. Ask them to write down the impression they have after reading the first two chapters and then read on. Let them log these again after several more chapters, before reading to the end and writing down the final assessment.

2. Character grid

Age range
Seven to eleven.

Group size
Small group (two to six children).

What you need
Copies of photocopiable page 157, pencils, a story with clear characters portrayed (at least one copy of the text between two children).

What to do
Let the group read the story, then decide on the main characters. Give each child a copy of photocopiable page 157 and ask them to write the

4. Make a board game

Age range
Seven to eleven.

Group size
Two to four children.

What you need
Copies of photocopiable page 159 or a large sheet of paper, felt-tipped pens, a short story that the group already know counters, die.

What to do
Explain to the children that they are going to design a board game based on the story. Ask the groups to decide which episodes were of major importance in the story.

Distribute copies of photocopiable page 159 and ask the children to adapt the game board, deciding which episodes of the story would warrant the player moving forward on the board and which would mean the player should be penalised (For example, 'Edmund gets into the witch's sleigh. Miss a turn.'). Ask them to plan where to put these 'penalty' squares on to the baseboard.

The children may wish to incorporate specific features into their design, for example, when players move forwards or backwards they should land on a square without any writing in.

Ask the children to complete the board game by writing in the chosen squares and illustrating the baseboard with appropriate drawings round the edges.

They can then play the game!

3. What did you think?

Age range
Seven to eleven.

Group size
Whole class working in pairs.

What you need
A story with good character portrayal, copies of photocopiable page 158, pencils.

What to do
Read the story as a class, then ask the children to decide which are the main characters.

Distribute copies of photocopiable page 158 and ask the children to list the main characters down the side of the sheet. Let the children work in pairs to fill in the columns.

Collect the results from each pair. Ask the children to add up the results. Display the grids with the book.

names of the characters down the side. Next ask them to write a selection of characteristics across the top of the sheet, either choosing from the list provided or contributing their own.

Next, ask the children to work as individuals to complete their own grids, either by putting a tick in the box or by awarding characters marks out of five. (The higher the mark, the stronger the characteristic displayed by that character.)

Ask the group to compare answers and discuss any discrepancies.

5. Write a reference

Age range
Seven to eleven.

Group size
Pairs.

What you need
One book per pair, copies of photocopiable page 160, pencils.

What to do
Ask each pair to select a character from their book and decide on a job for which that character might apply.

Give the children copies of photocopiable page 160 and ask them to write a job reference for the character.

Ask the pairs to swop references and decide whether they would interview the applicant after reading the other child's reference. Encourage them to develop 'mock' interviews, one child acting the part of the chosen character and the other child as the interviewer.

6. Author of the year

Age range
Eight to eleven.

Group size
Pairs or small groups.

What you need
Individual titles by different authors (if possible three or four books by each author).

What to do
Explain to the groups that they each have to choose the 'Author of the year' by looking at the different books the authors have written and judging which author they think is the best.

Ask the groups to take turns to justify their choice to the rest of the class, explaining why they rejected some authors and how they came to make their final choice.

Display some of the winning author's books in the book corner or library, together with a list of the reasons for the choice.

As a variation, different groups could select different 'awards', such as 'Illustrator of the year', 'Non-fiction writer of the year', 'Poet of the year' and 'Historical character of the year'.

CHAPTER 8

USSR

What is USSR?

USSR stands for Uninterrupted Sustained Silent Reading. Schools have different acronyms or names for this activity, but the common characteristic is that children spend time each day reading alone.

USSR is a relatively new phenomenon in our schools.

Indeed in 1979 Lunzer & Gardner were able to say, 'teachers regard reading in lesson time with some degree of suspicion. They feel uneasy if pupils are 'only reading'; they consider they may be regarded as inefficient if a visitor to a lesson finds a substantial number of pupils merely gazing at books or resource materials.' (The Effective Use of Reading, Heinemann, 1979.)

Opinions have considerably altered over the past decade and many schools now view a quiet reading time as an essential component of the school day.

BACKGROUND

Why USSR?

Schools may differ in the ways they choose to organise USSR but they all share the following basic reasons for including it in the school day.
• USSR gives children the opportunity to read at their own rate.
• USSR allows children plenty of experience in trying out books and finding those which suit their emotional and intellectual needs.
• USSR is vital because if quiet reading does not happen in schools it probably will not happen at all.
• USSR gives children the opportunity for undirected reading. It is through this kind of reading that preferences and dislikes about genres or authors are revealed.

The organisation of USSR

If USSR is being introduced in a school or class for the first time, there are certain issues to be considered.

How can I make time for USSR?

Many teachers of children aged seven to twelve find that a 20 or 30 minute quiet reading time can be enjoyed every day. Of course, if the idea of USSR is new to the school, teachers will have to consider carefully how to claim that time from the rest of the curriculum. Perhaps there has been library time which could now become part of USSR time; perhaps some of the time children have spent reading aloud to the teacher could be spent on USSR. Such issues need to be carefully considered and, if USSR is to be a school practice, then all the staff need to be involved.

What extra resources will I need?

The idea of USSR is that during quiet reading time children make their own reading selection. This material could range from a comic brought from home to a reading scheme book. The point is that the teacher does not dictate the reading material, unless the pupil brings obviously unsuitable material into the classroom.

This freedom of choice might have consequences both on book organisation and book selection in the school. If the bulk of the reading resources in the classroom are in the form of reading schemes then, undoubtedly, children are going to require a wider choice of material. This may mean a lot more children using the library. This, in turn, will have resourcing implications for the school as it will need to ensure that the library has enough books, both fiction and non-fiction, for *all* readers in the school.

Some schools organise resources into class libraries and if children are reading daily they will need quite a stock of books to satisfy all interests. This is likely to require considerable duplication of books as pupils across the classes will have both reading abilities and reading interests in common. It can be quite useful to keep books 'on the move' by swapping some of the stock from each class with the same number of books from a nearby class. If the library also has a stock of fiction books then these too need to be circulated to the class libraries.

What about those children who cannot read?

Such children still need the opportunity to look at books. It is not a waste of their time, even if their decoding skills are poor. Attempting to read as much as they can, remembering text they have heard read to them and interpreting pictures is all valuable experience. It is precisely what we would expect to do with the pre-school child and, in terms of their reading development, that is the stage these older poor readers have reached.

If these children can only read a text with adult support then there are considerable implications for the resources in the classroom and an obvious need for books with little or no text.

What should I tell the parents?

Parents should be informed about the school's decision to include quiet reading in the timetable. They will need to have the following benefits clearly explained to them.
• It enables children to practise the reading skills they have acquired.
• It encourages children to become 'hooked on books'.
• It puts the onus of interpretation firmly on the child's shoulders, instead of always relying on an adult listener.
• It encourages enjoyment and gives reading a purpose for children.

Does the session have to be absolutely silent?

It is probably best to strive for general quietness in the classroom rather than complete silence. The object is to have as few disturbances as possible. Some schools discourage pupils from using USSR time to change books. Instead they allocate time immediately prior to USSR during which children ensure that they have enough reading material to keep them occupied. Other schools find it difficult to spare this extra allocation of time so the choosing and changing of books happens during USSR.

What should the teacher do during USSR?

Ideally, teachers too should be reading during USSR, modelling the importance of reading for the children. It is quite possible that children will never see another adult reading in this way, so it is a much-needed example for them.

Some teachers feel sufficiently relaxed about this to bring their own reading material to school. Others use the time to extend their knowledge of the books available to children so that they can better recommend and advise children when they are making choices. However, there will be the days when pressure of work means it is quite impossible to relax and read during USSR. Whatever you do, try to maintain a general relaxed atmosphere during the session.

Do I need to keep a record of what children are reading during USSR?

You do not need to keep a record of what each child has read, but the children themselves should certainly do so. This record can take the form of a simple diary in which children note the title, author, date started/date finished and possibly some comment (eg 10/10 or 'Not as good as I thought it would be', and so on).

You might consider encouraging children to note whether the book was fiction or non-fiction. This information can be very useful in finding out the range of pupils' reading experiences. These reading diaries can form the basis for book conferences between children and between teacher and pupil. Photocopiable page 161 gives a suggested format of reading diary.

Aidan Chambers (1991) has identified four indispensable features of a successful reading environment for children in school:
• time for reading;
• well-chosen book stock;
• reading aloud to children;
• opportunities to respond to reading.
(Aidan Chambers *The Reading Environment*, Thimble Press, 1991)

Our goal is for children to have high expectations of books as sources of enjoyment and information; we need to give them the opportunity to discover that for themselves.

CHAPTER 9

Reading aloud

Reading aloud to the class is a commonplace activity in the early years at school, but many teachers of older pupils find that the school day is so crammed with other activities that there is no time to fit it in. It is often felt that once children have mastered certain early literacy skills, it is not so important to continue reading aloud to them. This chapter sets out to explain the value of reading aloud to children of all ages.

BACKGROUND

Why read aloud?

Many radio station schedules include stories being read aloud, and the majority of these are in adult listening time. This is presumably done not just to fill a gap in air-time but because there is consumer demand. Even in adulthood, hearing a good story well read can be a particular pleasure.

Reading aloud to children is not just a luxury which can be sacrificed for 'more important' things. Reading aloud gives the teacher the opportunity to convince pupils that all the effort they put into becoming a reader is worthwhile: the pay-off is being able to participate fully in the world of books.

Despite discouraging reports in the newspapers, most children do become competent readers. However, it is quite easy for their interest in reading to wane once the first enthusiasm for acquiring the skill passes. It is often difficult to continue to stimulate a developing interest in reading. One successful way is by teachers reading to pupils. This is the perfect role-model for children who might otherwise never witness an adult spending any length of time with books.

Reading a story aloud to the whole class provides the pupils with a model of how to read not only the words, but also features of written texts such as punctuation or voices with accents. The shared experience also provides the basis for discussion and opportunities for reflection to which everyone can contribute. This can result in a more wide-ranging discussion than arises from group reading discussion, as such groups are often composed of like-minded children of similar ability.

Problems

Every area of the curriculum offers opportunities for learning, coupled with organisational difficulties for the teacher. Reading aloud to the class is no exception.

..... And now, Reginald Thumper reads the second part of Thomas Hardy's "Far from the Madding Crowd".....

FLOUR

What about those children who read ahead?

Some keen readers will borrow from the library a copy of the book you are reading and will read ahead to the end of the story at a considerably faster pace than you can deliver it to the class! Most of those keen readers will also enjoy the story told at your pace, and their 'double read' will be very beneficial when it comes to class discussions. However, if you intend to do quite a lot of prediction work around the plot, and if the plot is quite a complex one where readers are kept guessing to the last page, then you may wish to ask children not to read ahead. Explain to the children why. You may find it useful to have other books by the same author to offer to those children to read during USSR times.

Often it really does not matter if some children are ahead of you in the story. Most will still like to accompany you as you read, even if their own bookmark is a chapter or so further along. It is important to remember that children enjoy re-reading and many choose to re-read books on a regular basis. Reading what has become familiar gives children the opportunity to reflect upon deeper meaning, as the actual words themselves present no barrier.

What about restless children?

Some children find it difficult to concentrate when only their ears are occupied! A television diet has made them associate stories and dramas with visual as well as auditory stimulation and, consequently, some of them find 'just listening' very difficult. It is a good idea to provide these fidgets with pages from a colouring book and some coloured pencils. (The Altair design colouring pads are excellent for this purpose, see Resources, page 192.) Colouring patterns engages restless fingers, but the story engages their minds. They should not attempt any more purposeful colouring, such as finishing a diagram for science which would require extra thought. It is sometimes possible to tell which are the most gripping parts of the story as the rate of colouring decreases as the children become absorbed in the plot!

How can I find books that will appeal to everyone?

This can be a dilemma and you won't be able to keep everyone happy all the time. If, however, you plan a programme of reading aloud it is much easier to persuade the listeners that, although this story might not at first appeal to them, they can be reassured that a subsequent choice will suit them perfectly.

The best titles for reading aloud do not obviously fall into categories headed 'Suitable for Boys' or 'Suitable for Girls'. Those are precisely the kinds of reading experiences junior aged children are discovering for themselves in their choice of private reading. A good read-aloud has something for everyone.

What should I read aloud?

Through reading aloud sessions, you can introduce children to texts that some may struggle with as a solo read. Indeed, it is probably unwise to use reading aloud sessions just to read books that many pupils might have selected for their own personal reading. The reading aloud sessions offer the opportunity to share texts which benefit from adult mediation and interpretation. They should represent a challenge for many readers in the class, not only in terms of the language difficulties of the text, but also in terms of the themes and issues raised by the plot.

Once you have read a story to the class, you will probably find that almost all of the children will then wish to read that story personally. Giving up your time to select and read a book will create a special

interest in that story for the pupils. This means that your selection of titles is very important (see page 84).

Giving children the opportunity to re-read stories can be important; it gives them a further chance to come to terms with the events of the plot and with the issues raised in the story. The stories chosen by a teacher are likely to etch themselves upon the minds of many of the class. It is not uncommon to meet adults who remember stories their class teacher read them when they were in primary school. This is a measure of how significant they found that experience. It would be a great shame if future generations did not have those memories because of other curriculum necessities.

Some teachers like to link fiction read aloud to a theme introduced elsewhere in the curriculum. This enables certain themes to be explored that provide interesting perspectives on a non-fiction topic.

Poetry makes an excellent read-aloud choice. Ideally, read-aloud poems should be either a longer narrative poem that is a story in itself, or a shorter poem that the children might try to learn by heart and say with you.

When should I read aloud?

Reading aloud sessions need to take place on a regular basis if children are to be convinced that teachers believe in the value of sharing books with them. Schools organise timetables in a number of ways and many options are available, for example:
• once a week for an extended period (eg. 40 minutes);
• twice a week for shorter sessions (eg. 20 minutes each);
• once a day (10 minutes).

These options can be arranged to suit the needs of timetables and to present most appropriately a particular story to the class. A longish novel with many characters and an involved plot is probably best read in thirty-minute slots. A short story anthology fits well into two twenty-minute slots in a week. A story with short chapters or a book with separate incidents linked by a common theme can be read in daily doses.

Some of the sessions would benefit from having time set aside to reflect upon what has been heard and to pool predictions about what might happen next (see Chapter 10, 'Book talk').

If finding this time for reading aloud on a regular basis is very difficult you might consider sacrificing one of the quiet reading sessions and using that time to read to children.

The benefits of reading aloud

When children are newly fluent at reading, they are still constantly paying attention to the decoding skills – to reading the words on the page.

Sometimes this gets in the way of the meaning of the words – the happiness described, the sadness, the fear. When someone else is responsible for the decoding, children are free to concentrate on that meaning. The more they become familiar with the 'message' of reading, the more likely they are to apply it when they are reading privately.

Reading aloud regularly to children 'demands a great investment of time. Yet there is hardly any other investment, hardly any other area of study, that yields so potent a means of making literature live for children.' (Clark Sayers, 1973.)

Collections of short stories

A Place for Owls, Katherine McKeever, Cambridge, 1987.
Did I Ever Tell You...? Series, Iris Grender, Hutchinson.
Fingers Crossed, ed. Chris Powling, Knight Books, 1988.
Ghosts that Haunt You, ed. Aidan Chambers, Puffin, 1983.
Highdays and Holidays, ed. Eileen Colwell, Viking, 1988.
Imagine That!, Stephen and Sara Corrin, Puffin, 1988.
I'm Trying to Tell You, Bernard Ashley, Puffin, 1982.
The King of the Copper Mountain, Paul Biegel, Lion Books, 1990.
The Last Slice of Rainbow and Other Stories, Joan Aiken, Puffin, 1988.
Mouth Open, Story Jump Out, Grace Hallworth, Methuen, 1987.
The New Golden Land Anthology, ed. J. Elkin, Puffin, 1984.

Stories from Codling Village, Susan Hill, Julia MacRae, 1988.
The Storyteller, Anthony Minghella, Boxtree/TVS, 1988.
Tales for Telling, ed. Leila Berg, Methuen, 1983.
Till Owlyglass, Michael Rosen, Walker, 1991.
Timepieces – a Year in the Life of a Suffolk Village, David Leney, Dent, 1989.

Good novels to read aloud

7 – 9 years
A Little Dog Like You, Rosemary Sutcliff, Orchard, 1987.
Barty, Janet Collins, Magnet, 1987.
Danny Fox, David Thomson, Puffin, 1971.
Fred the Angel, Martin Waddell, Young Lions, 1990.
Olga da Polga, Michael Bond, Puffin, 1983.
The Real Thief, William Steig, Faber, 1990.
Stuart Little, E.B. White, Young Lions, 1989.

The Toby Man, Dick King-Smith, Gollancz, 1989.
The Wilds of Whip-Poor-Will Farm, Janet Foster, Cambridge, 1987.

9 – 11 years
A Great Escape, Colin Dann, Red Fox, 1990.
A Taste of Blackberries, D. Buchanon Smith, Puffin, 1990.
Gaffer Samson's Luck, Jill Paton Walsh, Puffin, 1987.
How's Business?, Alison Prince, Andre Deutsch, 1987.
The Indian in the Cupboard, Lynne Reid Banks, Mayflower, 1981.
On My Honour, Marion Dane Bauer, Puffin, 1988.
The Seventeenth Swap, Eloise Jarvis McGraw, Viking, 1988.
Thunder and Lightnings, Jan Mark, Puffin, 1978.
Tom's Amazing Machine, Gordon Snell, Beaver, 1989.
Underground to Canada, Barbara Claassen Smucker, Puffin, 1978.
The Whipping Boy, Sid Fleischman, Magnet, 1988.

CHAPTER 10

Book talk

It is possible for children in Y3 to Y6 to become reasonably proficient word readers but not necessarily readers who actively and continuously process what they read. As one eight-year-old girl was heard to say, 'Sometimes my mouth says the words but my head does not follow.' The processing of what we read takes many forms. It may be an intellectual response where we take on board new knowledge and use it to interpret facts. It may be an affective response where we live in the world of the book and are emotionally moved by what we read. These two responses are the main reasons why adults are drawn to books. In the classroom it is the teacher's role to provide children with reading experiences which offer satisfaction both intellectually and emotionally.

BACKGROUND

Reading is usually a solitary experience. For naturally gregarious children it may be the only school activity they perform without peer support. For some children this escape into privacy provided by reading is a welcome release from the pressures of school life. Indeed, most classes have one or two 'bookworms' who snatch every possible moment to disappear in the world of books.

However, this does not apply to most children and we often need to engineer situations in which the quiet times of solitary reading are matched by sessions when children share their responses to that reading. For some children this can become a motive for reading in itself. It also provides a focus for less certain readers, knowing that they will be expected to respond to what they have read.

A persistent search for meaning

Encouraging children to discuss what they have read helps them to reflect upon what they have understood about it. In his book *Book Talk* (1985) Aidan Chambers describes talking about books as 'the three sharings'. He suggests that during book talk there can be:
• a sharing of enthusiasm;
• a sharing of puzzles;
• a sharing of connections.

At first, children may use book talk sessions to share their enthusiasms, for example, reading out the funny bits. However, children can also be encouraged to use book talk sessions to raise queries about aspects of the plot they may have found confusing. This may be because they haven't understood some of the words, or because the book explores issues with which they are unfamiliar. Book talk sessions can help clarify matters, enabling children to interpret the new ideas in the book in the light of the experiences of others.

Book talk sessions also help children to make connections between books and authors, and open the door to interpreting one story in terms of other stories read. This helps children to become critically aware of the role of the author and it will undoubtedly help them in their own writing.

Discussion also gives readers a chance to reconsider their initial responses and opinions. Book talk helps children to realise that there may be many interpretations of the same text. They learn to explain their opinions and to justify them through reference both to the book and to other experiences. In this way children develop as critical readers; they learn to appreciate that it is acceptable to have differing opinions and that all opinions may be valid.

Organising book talk sessions

Book talk may be introduced as a whole-class activity but it is usually much more successful undertaken in small groups. The children may choose to read the text privately and agree to come together, either at the end of the story or at some agreed midway point. It is a good idea to have a set of open-ended questions ready to form the basis of the discussion. For example:
• Can you follow the plot?
• With which character do you identify most closely?
• What do you think of the story so far?
• What do you think will happen next?

Encourage the children to respond with their opinions supported by references to the text, for example, 'I got a bit lost when...' or 'The character I like best is... because she...'

Make sure that you give plenty of guidance for discussion until the children are used to such sessions. However, once book talk becomes an established part of the reading curriculum, children should be able to organise the activity for themselves.

Book talk sessions encourage children to question what they are reading – they begin to see implied meanings and they draw inferences. Some children would, of course, do all these things without the support of the group, but many young readers would not go further than the words of the page without such a focus.

Which resources are best for book talk?

When introducing book talk into a classroom it is often best to start from an enjoyable but not necessarily demanding reading experience, for example, picture books. One of the greatest advantages of using picture books is that they enable children of all reading abilities to participate. Those children who find reading difficult may find particular benefit from such sessions. Because there is usually only a limited amount of text in a picture book the words can be read quickly and then time can be spent discussing the meaning. With picture books, the meaning of the words is enhanced through interpretation of the illustration. For this activity to be successful there should be multiple copies of picture books available.

Books suitable for book talk

Burningham, John (1991) *Aldo*, Cape.
Varley, Susan (1985) *Badger's Parting Gifts*, Picture Lions.
Oakley, Graham (1989) *The Diary of a Church Mouse*, Macmillan.
Richardson, Jean (1989) *A Dog for Ben*, Puffin.
Cole, Babette (1991) *Hurrah for Ethelyn*, Heinemann.
Wilhelm, Hans (1986) *I'll Always Love You*, Knight.
Ahlberg, Janet and Allan (1986) *The Jolly Postman*, Heinemann.
Hedderwick, Mairi (1988) *Katie Morag and the Two Grandmothers*, Picture Lions.
Munsch, Robert (1982) *The Paper Bag Princess*, Hippo.
Scieszka, Jon (1990) *The True Story of the Three Little Pigs*, Viking Kestrel.

ACTIVITIES

1. Picture response

Age range
Seven to twelve.

Group size
Four to five children.

What you need
Multiple copies of picture books (see recommended list at the end of Chapter 3), 'Reading fiction', or further suggestions of titles on page 92).

What to do
Give each child a copy of the chosen book. Ask them to look carefully at the pictures and to comment upon them. They might like to make comparisons between one illustration and another later in the book. Children can be surprisingly perceptive about details in illustrations. For example, when looking at Maurice Sendak's book *Outside Over There*, a girl in a Y4 class suggested that the different colours used in the illustrations represented the different moods of the characters.

It might be necessary to probe for some responses, for example:
• What do you think that character is thinking?
• If you could add a speech bubble, what do you think that character would say?
• Is there anything in this illustration that makes you feel happy/sad/angry etc?

2. What's the difference?

Age range
Seven to twelve.

Group size
Five to six children.

What you need
Multiple copies of a picture book.

What to do
Give each child in the group a copy of the story and, after the children have read the words, ask them to study the pictures. Encourage them to consider whether the words and pictures differ. Are the illustrations pictorial representations of the words, or do the pictures take the story further?

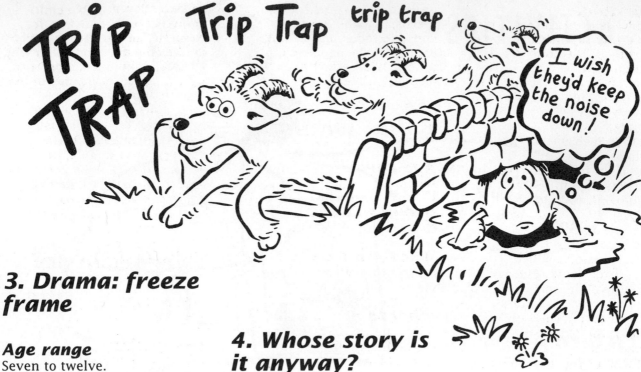

3. Drama: freeze frame

Age range
Seven to twelve.

Group size
Five to six children.

What you need
Multiple copies of a picture book.

What to do
Give each group a copy of the book. Let them read the story, then ask them to choose *one* of the illustrations to depict as a tableau. If necessary, the children can choose to represent two pictures to give each child the opportunity to play a role.

Once they have formed the tableau, ask them in turn to say *one* line 'in character'. This does not have to reflect the actual text but should be the child's interpretation of that character in that particular stance.

Ask the children to perform their tableaux to the rest of the class and let the others guess the characters shown.

4. Whose story is it anyway?

Age range
Seven to twelve.

Group size
Five to six children.

What you need
Multiple copies of a picture book.

What to do
After reading the story, ask the children to identify the main characters and decide from whose perspective the story is told. For example, in *Little Red Riding Hood*, the girl is at the centre of the plot.

Ask the groups of children to consider the plot from a different character's point of view. For example, in *Little Red Riding Hood*, the children may choose the wolf. Perhaps the wood-cutter had been cutting down the forest where the wolf lived and destroying his natural habitat and source of food, so the wolf was driven to eating grandmothers through desperation!

Conclude the activity by asking the groups to share their different perspectives or by letting the children make a case for defending a 'bad' character, such as Jack's giant or the troll in *The Three Billy Goats Gruff*.

5. What's going on?

Age range
Seven to twelve.

Group size
Whole class, working in groups of five to six children.

What you need
Multiple copies of a picture book, pencils, paper.

What to do

Read the story together, with each group following the text in a copy of the book. Ask the children to reflect upon the action of the book. It might be quite useful to write this down in a very simple form. For example:

• Mother Bear makes the porridge.
• The porridge is too hot.
• The Bears go for a walk.
• *Meanwhile* Goldilocks arrives.
• She eats the porridge.
• She breaks the chair.
• She sleeps on the bed.
• The Three Bears return.

Ask the children to consider what the other characters might be doing while the main action of the story is unfolded. For example:
• What did the Three Bears do on their walk?
• What is Goldilocks' mother doing while her daughter is away?

When the children are familiar with this activity they could extend it further by discussing why the author chose to focus upon some actions at the expense of others. What effect does this have upon the story?

6. Hot seating

Age range
Seven to twelve.

Group size
Five to six children.

What you need
Multiple copies of a picture book.

What to do
Allow the children time to read the book and discuss the contents. Ask each child to choose the character they would most like to be. Let each child in turn present himself as that character while the others ask him questions.

Encourage the child in the 'hot seat' to answer 'in character' as far as possible. If the text supplies an answer to the question then the child should give that answer, for example, an Ugly Sister might answer the question about why she was unkind to Cinderella by saying, 'I was jealous of her beauty.' However, if the questions cannot be answered by the text the child must answer in an appropriate manner. For example, in answer to a question about the food at the ball, 'Cinderella' could choose whatever culinary delights she fancies.

7. Who can go?

Age range
Seven to twelve.

Group size
Five to six children.

What you need
Multiple copies of a picture book.

What to do
After reading the picture book, ask the children to discuss whether any characters could be removed from the story without it affecting the plot. If not, why are they included?

Ask the children to consider what the plot would be like without one of the main characters. For example, what would the story of the Billy Goats Gruff be like without the troll?

What did you think when your son Jack brought home the magic beans?

8. Looking at language

Age range
Eight to twelve.

Group size
Five to six children.

What you need
Multiple copies of a picture book.

What to do
After the group have read the book, ask them to reflect upon the actual words used to tell the story. Are some words particularly good? Do they really help the reader to visualise the scene? Are there any comparisons made that are particularly convincing?

This is a good opportunity to talk about similes and metaphors, for example, *I Want a Cat* by Tony Ross: 'It was like a million pigs falling downstairs, and the neighbours banging on the front door.'

9. Connections

Age range
Eight to twelve.

Group size
Five to six children.

What you need
Approximately four picture books with similar subject matter. For example:

Cats
Fred, Posy Simmonds, Picture Puffin, 1989.
I Want a Cat, Tony Ross, Andersen Press, 1989.
Slobcat, Paul Geraghty, Hutchinson, 1991.
Our Cat Flossie, Ruth Brown, Beaver, 1987.

Families
Five Minutes Peace, Jill Murphy, Walker Books, 1986.
I'll Take You to Mrs Cole! Nigel Gray, Picturemac, 1987.
Not Now, Bernard, David McKee, Beaver Books, 1987.
Piggy Book, Anthony Browne, Julia MacRae, 1987.

Conservation
The World that Jack Built, Ruth Brown, Andersen Press, 1990.
Oi! Get Off Our Train, John Burningham, Jonathan Cape, 1989.
Where the Forest Meets the Sea, Jeannie Baker, Julia MacRae, 1991.
Window, Jeannie Baker, Julia MacRae, 1988.

What to do
Ask the group to read all the books and discuss the different ways in which the theme is portrayed. Does the group have a favourite book out of the four? Does one book deal with certain aspects better than the others? If so, how?

CHAPTER 11

Reading and writing

Traditionally, reading and writing have been taught separately. Children expected times when they 'did' writing-based activities, such as creative writing or comprehension and grammar exercises, and these learning experiences were quite separate from reading-based activities, such as private reading or reading aloud sessions.

Of course, teachers realised that children who read widely were generally more confident when it came to composing their own texts, but few teachers capitalised upon this. Recent critical thinking about writing (prompted by The National Writing Project) sees it as a process which cannot be separated from reading; it is through writing that children come to consolidate their reading, and it is through reading that children learn the skills of writing.

The act of reading requires us first to decode what a writer has written and then to encode the meaning. When we write we construct a meaning through words which we hope the reader will reconstruct. It is therefore through writing that we can best appreciate the needs of the reader.

Reading and writing are thus interconnected skills. The problem facing the teacher is how to apply this in the classroom.

Questionnaire
What books do you like to read?
What sort of pictures do you like?
Who is your favourite author?
What is your f
How m eac
Why do

Hissing and glistening
the snake slithers by
shiny and slippery
scary in the grass

A Plant
Leaf
Vein
bud
stem
root hairs
roots

Emma's Pony

Sometimes Barney bullied bear.

Sometimes they were the best of friends

Journey into Space
Once upon a time there was a boy called Dean who was to be a brilliant footballer and wanted to be a spaceman so he made a rocket out of some bits of metal out of the garage and set off into space in the rocket and then he went to Pluto and landed on a million heads and a million ain out at him and eat you

and then the monster was dead in a big pool of blood and Dean went home for his tea
The End.

VIKINGS

OPEN DAY
SCHOOL WILL BE OPEN TO THE PUBLIC ON
14th June
9:00 am to 7:30 pm
1one welcome

BACKGROUND

The National Curriculum for English expects children at Key Stage 2 to become familiar with reading and writing in a variety of styles. This is best achieved not only by reading examples of particular genres but by recreating that genre as a writer. It is therefore important to organise the reading experience in a cycle of learning which involves:
• *talking* about texts;
• *reading* related texts;
• *writing* similar texts.

Talking and reading about a subject is essential background to writing about it. This learning cycle – talking/reading/talking/writing/talking – is the basis for successful learning. It is epitomised by the maxim, 'if you want to learn – teach'. Communicating to others what you have learned helps to retain the facts and personalise the knowledge.

Encouraging children to use texts as models for their own writing is a very valuable teaching strategy; indeed, it is the only way for children to become confident writers in a variety of styles.

In the same way that we as adults might do background reading about an author's novels and critiques of that author's work, as well as talking through our ideas before attempting to write our own critical essay, so we can encourage children to go through similar procedures before producing a particular piece of writing for a purpose.

Children should read, write and discuss all of the following genres in order to gain an understanding of reading and writing for the different purposes.
• Personal writing, such as diaries, journals and letters.
• Narrative texts, including adventure, mystery, fairy tales and science fiction.
• Expository texts, such as diaries, journals and letters.
• Poetry and plays, including different poetic forms, from ballads to free verse.
• Instruction, such as on labels, directions, reports and diagrams.

A range of such texts will be needed as models – it is insufficient to have only one example of each. For example, a variety of dictionaries is essential, from the simple illustrated dictionary to full-scale adult dictionaries; also different kinds of non-fiction texts, from short factual entries randomly placed over a page, to heftier tomes giving more specific information on a subject.

These genres are not exclusive to the English Curriculum, they could easily be included in the range of texts more specifically applied to other areas of the curriculum. For example:
• reports: science;
• instruction: maths, technology;
• diagrams: geography;
• diaries: history;
• labels: science diagrams.

ACTIVITIES

1. Making an encyclopaedia

Age range
Any age.

Group size
Whole class, working individually or in pairs.

What you need
An example of an encyclopaedia, large (A3) sheets of card, large sheets of paper, pencils, felt-tipped pens, adhesive, stapler or hole punch and ribbon.

What to do
Explain to the class that they are going to make an encyclopaedia for the topic they have just completed. (The class needs to have covered a topic in some detail so that individuals or pairs can select a particular aspect.) Demonstrate how an encyclopaedia works. Show the children the contents list, the guide words, the alphabetical order, the index, the variety of authors, and so on.

Ask the children to work either in pairs or alone and select an aspect of the topic they have just completed to make into an entry for the encyclopaedia. Check that their selections cover the major aspects of the topic and advise on different choices if necessary.

Ask the children to plan their entry. Demonstrate that the sentences need to be succinct and any illustration has to be informative – maybe a map, diagram or drawing.

When entries have been written, the class should collect them together, then place them in alphabetical order.

Each child should also write a contents heading and select words from the entry for an index.

Divide the children into groups and allocate the following activities:
• organising the title page;
• organising the contents page;
• arranging the alphabetically ordered entries on to the large sheets of paper;
• organising the index;
• organising the guide words at the head of each sheet;
• devising the front and back covers;
• binding the encylopaedia.

The finished encyclopaedia can be put in the book corner for future reference.

Take three steps towards the clock, then turn to face Mr. Edwards' chair.

2. Write a letter

Age range
Any age.

Group size
Whole class, working in pairs.

What you need
Examples of 'official letters' (such as those in *The Jolly Postman* by Janet and Allan Ahlberg, letters to the press, letters from the council or standard letters from banks), pencils, paper.

What to do
Before the activity, prepare a letter to the children concerning, for example, an environmental issue and using 'official' language.

Read the class a selection of 'official' letters and talk about the language used.

Then read to the class the letter you have written them. Discuss with them how they could reply to the letter. How could they write this in a suitable style?

Divide the group into pairs and ask them to reply.

Read the replies aloud and discuss with the whole class the relative merits of their replies.

Display your original letter and the replies on the wall.

3. Find the treasure

Age range
Any age.

Group size
Whole class, working in pairs or fours.

What you need
An area of classroom or school in which to hide some 'treasure', paper, pencil, some 'treasure' (such as a small toy).

What to do
Before the activity, hide the 'treasure' and write instructions for the treasure seekers to follow.

Divide the class into pairs or fours.

Allow the first group to follow the instructions until they find the 'treasure'. Then ask them to select a new hiding place for the treasure, and to write new instructions, using the original instructions as a model, to give to the next group.

When all the groups have had a turn, discuss with the whole class which instructions they found the easiest to follow and which they found the most difficult. Could these have been expressed more clearly?

4. Character characteristics

Age range
Any age.

Group size
Whole class, working in pairs.

What you need
A book containing a particularly clear description of a character, paper, felt-tipped pens.

What to do
Prepare for the activity by making enough copies of the descriptive passage for the pairs of children to have one each. Read the passage to the class. Ask the children to tell you which words they think describe the appearance of the character, and which words they think describe the behaviour and thoughts of the character.

Give each pair a copy of the passage and ask them to underline in different colours the different types of words and phrases the author has used to describe the character. For example, they could use red to underline all the words which describe a character's appearance, and blue to underline all the words used to describe his behaviour.

Ask the children to invent a character and write about him in a similar way. Ensure that they include all the physical characteristics.

Let them write out these descriptions and exchange them with the other pairs.

Further activities
• Ask each pair to 'act' the character while the rest of the class describe his behaviour and what they think the character looks like.
• Select a passage from a book which describes a place and, using the same procedure, ask the children to identify all the words which describe either the atmosphere or the action that is taking place.

5. Choose a word

Age range
Any age.

Group size
Whole class working individually.

What you need
Copies of photocopiable page 162, pencils, a copy of *Great Expectations* by Charles Dickens.

What to do
Give copies of photocopiable page 162 to the children. (Alternatively, devise your own descriptive passage with the adjectives/adverbs deleted. These should be selected in sufficient number so that the child can read the passage without loss of meaning. The younger child is likely to need more text between deletions than the older reader.)

Ask them to read through the whole passage before they begin to fill in the missing words as far as they are able. Share these suggestions with the whole class and discuss why some words may be more suitable than others.

Show the group the original text from *Great Expectations*. Why do they think the author chose certain words? Were any of their suggestions better or worse than the author's?

Further activity
Let the children write their own descriptions with deleted words for their peers to try to complete.

CHAPTER 12

Hearing children read

Hearing children read has traditionally been considered the single most important activity that a teacher does to ensure that they develop as readers. The teacher was expected to hear all children read every day. In reality this was almost impossible to achieve and so as children became 'free readers' (that is, 'finished' the reading scheme) it was presumed that they could now read proficiently and that it was no longer necessary to hear them. Their progress, if monitored at all, was judged either by the number of reading books with which

they were provided (and these were expected to last them through the primary years) or by having a class 'reader' from which each child read aloud in turn. This usually meant that good readers read ahead, or even had a second book under the desk, and the poor readers publicly struggled in front of the rest of the class.

In the late 1970s research undertaken by Manchester University (Southgate, 1976) looking at average readers of seven years found that children who were heard to read less often but for a

longer time generally made better progress than those who were heard to read every day. At the same time Kenneth Goodman began research in the USA into the 'miscues' that children made when they read aloud. These findings also confirmed that teachers who listened to their pupils read a considerable amount of text and recorded the miscues (deviations from the written text) were better able to assess and diagnose the reading needs of their pupils.

Andrew opened the wooden box and took out a yellowed piece of paper...

BACKGROUND

Why hear children read aloud?

The main reason for hearing children read is to ensure that they are making progress and that they employ useful strategies when they meet unrecognised vocabulary. Obviously the most important aspect of reading is to understand the text and so discussion with the child is also necessary in order to check that she is not simply decoding efficiently.

How often should a child be heard to read?

This varies according to the ability of the individual children and, realistically, the more able readers are likely to be heard less often. However, schools do need to address this issue and offer guidelines to all the staff. It is very tempting to believe that the avid silent reader in the class is coping and does not need to be heard on a regular basis. It may only take place a few times each term, but it should happen.

The avid readers in any class are fairly easy to identify and the attitude they have towards books, snatching the odd moment just to read a few more pages, can disguise some possible poor reading strategies. These children need to be heard on a regular basis, reading from a wide range of genres and for longer than the statutory 'two minutes'. These able readers should not be ignored simply because the needs of others seem so much greater.

Average readers form the bulk of the pupils in every classroom. These children may appear to be coping with the reading offered in both fiction and non-fiction but they do not turn readily to books. They need constant reminders to maintain a regular reading experience. As they become more proficient silent readers it is all too easy for them to slip into the belief that being able to 'sound the words' inside their heads is all that is necessary. (As adults, we often do this when we are tired or when the subject matter is particularly difficult.)

Is this reading? These children need to emulate the avid reader, they need to *talk* about what they have read, they need to *share* the knowledge with their peers and adults, and they need to *be constantly shown* the value of reading for itself. It is important to keep a careful eye on how these children respond to texts. The main way to do this is to hear them read on a regular basis and to spend time discussing the books with them (see Chapter 7, 'Group reading'). It is all too easy for these children to appear confident, to read aloud quite rapidly and with intonation and expression, but this 'surface' read is as far as they go. They do not respond to the content and find it difficult to do more than a skimpy retelling of the text. It is essential to find time to share books with these children on a regular basis, at least once a fortnight with the younger child (Y3 to Y4) and monthly with the older pupils.

In most classes there are likely to be some children struggling with reading. As they grow older, the gap between them and their peers widens and they become dispirited and apathetic, frequently trying to avoid

reading altogether. These children demand an enormous amount of time, but hearing them read as often as possible may not be the most effective use of this time. Certainly you need to diagnose and monitor these children but hearing them read two or three times a week can mask the progress they are making. It may be more effective to set aside a regular weekly or even fortnightly teacher assessment session, while providing other regular and frequent opportunities for these children to practise reading, perhaps with peers, helpers or parents.

Characteristics of readers

C.M. Charles (1980) described three kinds of learners likely to be found in any class. These characteristics are not necessarily attributable to the ability of the learner but describe how they approach learning.

The adventurers
• These are active pupils who are eager to try out any new activity.
• They are initially enthusiastic, but this easily wanes as another subject takes their interest.
• They appear to know what they want to read and begin any new book with enthusiasm but all too often they fail to finish it, or they skip such large chunks that they only get a very superficial idea of the story.
• These readers are good at leaving out words they do not recognise and reading on, but they rarely return to that word later and do not seem perturbed that they did not quite understand.
• These children do not pay close attention to detail although they often work very creatively.

The ponderers
• These children start slowly but persevere for longer.
• They may continue with a book that they do not enjoy but they like to finish things.
• They pay close attention to detail and are very concerned to 'get things right'.
• They need encouragement to read on if they do not understand or recognise a word but they will return to it later, checking to see if they have understood it.
• These children usually produce high quality work, albeit rather slowly.
• In retelling a story they recall all the episodes and often give such a detailed report that it seems as though they are reading rather than using their own words!

The drifters
• These children are easily distracted and need constant teacher intervention to keep on task.

- They like the physical presence of the teacher for any task and constantly require support and encouragement.
- These children like to have a very clear idea of what is wanted in any activity and rarely deviate in an imaginative way from the task set.
- They like to be told which books to read, they read only as far as it has been suggested they might like to go and no further, no matter how interesting or exciting the text.
- Above all they like routines and will always follow these, sometimes inappropriately.

These characteristics are not dependent upon a pupil's reading ability and it is possible to find drifters among those who are apparently avid readers, and adventurers among the poor readers. Children need to be shown the importance of achieving a balance to learn when to be adventurous, when to ponder and even when to drift.

Listening to children read

Generally the teacher will take time to hear a child read and discuss the material in order to check that all is well and that the child is reading material appropriate to his reading ability. Occasionally the teacher will set time aside to do a detailed and diagnostic assessment on the 'miscues' that the reader is making. This is a time-consuming task and is unlikely to be carried out more than once a term, but it is worthwhile – not only in order to help the reader but also as part of that child's record.

Simplified miscue analysis

Using a tape recorder

Taping a child reading in a busy classroom may sound daunting, but in reality it is not too difficult and the results are extremely worthwhile. Bear in mind the following points.
- Taping a child does not mean that you and the child need to be isolated from the rest of the class.
- A simple recorder that has record, rewind, fast forward and an inbuilt microphone is

all that is needed. It doesn't need to be of high quality, just easy to use.

• The child needs to sit so that her voice is directed at the inbuilt mike. It is often better if the child sits with her back to a wall with the tape recorder placed in front and slightly tilted so that the voice hits the microphone rather than floats over the top. This positioning does not exclude all extraneous noise, but unless she whispers the child's voice can be clearly heard. (You should also remember that it will also record your voice, even if you are away from the microphone!)

• Although it may be more economical to plug the recorder into an electrical socket, make sure that you can also use it with batteries. This will allow you to be freer with your choice of venue.

• You can use a C60 or C90 cassette, using the same tape to keep an individual's record over many years. However, you may find it easier to use a C10 or C30, starting each recording at the beginning of a new tape.

• Many teachers keep both the tape and a copy of the relevant text as part of the reading profile.

• Taping the child means that you can mark the miscues away from the reading session. Although taking a 'running record' in Y2 classes has not been shown to be significantly interruptive, junior children are more likely to be concerned by the teacher marking a text while they read and could find this very distracting.

Coding the miscues

Figure 1 shows how miscues can be recorded on the text. The most important of these miscues are substitutions because it is through these that you are able to get an idea of what strategies the reader is using. These substitutions tend to fall into four categories.

• Graphic: the word substituted looks like the original.

• Phonic: the word substituted starts with the same sound as the word written.

• Syntactic: the substitution is grammatically correct, so a noun is substituted for a noun, adverb for adverb, etc.

• Semantic: the meaning of the original word is retained, eg. little for small.

Moon (1991) suggests a

Pause or hesitation: The girl was running|quickly down the|winding road.

Non response/refusal: The girl was running ~~quickly~~ down the winding road.

Omission: The girl was running ~~quickly~~ down the winding road.

Substitution: The girl was running ~~quickly~~ *quietly* down the winding road.

Insertion: The girl was running *very* quickly down the winding road.

Reversals: The girl was running quickly down the winding road, or,
The girl was running quickly down the winding road.

Repetition: The girl was running quickly down the winding road.

Self-correction: The girl was running quickly *quietly s.c.* down the winding road.

Ignores punctuation: The girl was running quickly down the winding road. She could hear the footsteps getting closer, but she...

Figure 1

formula for deciding whether the reader is at an independent, instructive or frustrational level. He adds the number of words refused to the number of substitutions that lost the meaning of the passage. This total is put over the number of words read (Figure 2).

However, by paying careful attention to the form of substitution and also assessing the discussion that follows, you will generally be able to decide the level that the child is on without having to indulge in mathematical activities. Remember, often one error sparks off others which would not normally have occurred. If you are not recording the child's reading and there

seems to be such a progression of miscues, intervene and take the reader back to the initial problem area. The reader will usually resume a more confident path if told the problem word or phrase and then allowed to continue. However, if the passage as a whole is too difficult then this help is unlikely to iron out the problem and further miscues will occur. This would obviously indicate that the reader is at frustration level and that the text is unsuitable. When this occurs it is impossible to get an accurate picture of the child as a reader

because all the miscues are present – hesitation, omissions, refusals, etc. If the child is recording the read and notices that it is going 'wrong', persuade him to turn off the tape and come and see you.

Choosing the right text

If the reader has chosen a text that is really too simple for her, then it is possible that no significant miscues occur. In this case you may wish to offer the reader a slightly harder text.

With confident silent readers there is the possibility of further complications. These children often want to put on a 'public performance read' for the teacher. They read with

$$\frac{\text{refusals} + \text{loss of meaning}}{\text{number of words in passage}} \times 100 = ?\%$$

1% = independent level
5% = instructional level
10% = frustrational level

Figure 2

intonation, expression and pace, but they rarely process the text at the same time. (It is similar to sight reading a piece of music – the concentration is on playing the right notes but it is possible for the player not to hear the tune!) If the child is then asked to discuss or retell the story, she is often unable to. It is often better for such children to be allowed to read the text for themselves first. This allows them time to 'digest' the content and separates them from the genuine 'non-comprehenders'.

In conclusion, it is best not to use books children read with ease and confidence for a diagnostic assessment. Texts which produce about five per cent of miscues are best – enough to analyse without disturbing the meaning. Although this sounds difficult to gauge, in fact almost every recording exposes some information. Text selection does become easier through practice.

Assessing the retelling

Asking the children to retell in their own words the story or passage they have just read is by far the most common 'check' that you are likely to make in order to see that they have read with understanding.

However, *how* the child retells can vary enormously and different levels of internalisation can be diagnosed. Although the oral performance is generally seen as the most important activity for assessment, it is the process of retelling that is likely to elicit to what extent the child understood what he was reading.

Stage 1 recall
The reader remembers the skeleton outline of the story but may retell it out of sequence. There are gaps in the content and usually long pauses and 'ums'. When asked an open-ended question the reader frequently looks very puzzled.

Stage 2 recall
The reader remembers most of the events and retells them in sequential order. He does not elaborate on the story. He gives little response to open-ended questions.

Stage 3 recall
Here the reader not only remembers the story in sequential order but often elaborates upon it, makes

remarks and spontaneously analogises with comments as to what he would have done in the same situation.

Stage 1 structure
The child often retells at great length a small incident in the story and this tends to distort the structure. Frequently the child emphasises either the opening or ending of the story but misses the complication in the plot that really was the point of the story. The retelling is given in brief phrases interspersed with 'you know' and many hand movements which the reader hopes the teacher will interpret.

Stage 2 structure
The main structure of the story is retained. The events are sequenced correctly and there is some evidence of linking one event to the next. The child may use 'then' frequently to link one event to the next. He may still miss out some important relationships within the text but the main episodes that are essential to the plot are present.

Stage 3 structure
This is a clear retelling with good cohesion. The child relates the episodes in the correct sequence but also conveys the relative importance of these episodes.

He sometimes makes remarks such as 'I thought the wolf would come but first such and such happened and then...'

Stage 1 response
This reader offers no comment upon the text. He does not link it with anything that may have occurred in his life or link it to similar stories or episodes in other books. He makes no evaluation of the characters and often seems puzzled when asked if he knows anyone like so-and-so in the story. He has to have irony pointed out to him.

Stage 2 response
This reader will make some evaluative comment on the story but is unable to say why he likes or dislikes the text. He

can recall the characters but is hazy about how he feels about them. Often the most he offers is that the character was 'naughty, bad or silly' but he cannot justify this with reference to the text.

Stage 3 response
This child spontaneously comments upon the text and characters. He sometimes talks about the author, linking this story to another where the author has used a similar situation or set of characters (for example, C.S. Lewis in the Narnia books, where Edmund improves in his character as he matures). This reader will refer back to episodes in other books and notice the development of the character. He identifies with the characters and frequently sympathises with both their situation and solution. He recognises metaphor and irony, often elaborating upon the 'joke' that the author has included by commenting 'you think that... is going to happen but...' or 'The author says this, but if you look at the pictures he really is like this.'

Children need as much careful and structured help with the retelling or response to what they have read as they do for the strategies they have used when reading aloud. If the sequence is going awry then the child needs to be encouraged to look at the story again to check what happened. They frequently need a model for the retelling of a story and also to listen to the kind of evaluation and appreciation that you make. It is not a spontaneous response, children need guidance, help and practice.

All the following activities have been designed to encourage children to recall and confidently retell texts they have read.

ACTIVITIES

1. Select six

Age range
Six to twelve.

Group size
Whole class working in smaller groups.

What you need
A short story or traditional tale, whiteboard, pens, large sheets of paper, pencils, paints.

What to do
Read either a short story or a traditional tale to the class. Tell the children to imagine that they have to commission six pictures to illustrate the story.

Collect ideas from the class as to which episodes they think should be illustrated. Write these down as they suggest them. Discuss with the children any offerings that have suggested the same episodes and take out any repetitions.

Ask the class to sequence the suggestions according to the story. (There may be more illustrations than the planned six at this point.)

Ask the class to select the 'best' six. Encourage the children to pick those which make a good story sequence, which could be used to retell the story in pictures, for example.

Divide the class into six groups. Ask them to select one picture topic each and to draw or paint it on to a large sheet of paper. When the pictures are finished, mount them on the classroom wall or make them into a 'big book' for all to use.

Variations
• Ask the groups to add a single line caption under their picture to summarise the story episode they are illustrating.
• Let the groups act out their episode in mime while the audience guesses which episode they are miming.

2. Storyboards

Age range
Six to twelve.

Group size
Whole class.

What you need
Short story, copies of photocopiable pages 163 and 164 (these are provided in two levels), pencils.

What to do
Either read a short story to the class or ask an individual child to select and read a short story.

Explain to the children how a film producer plans the plot and setting of a film on a storyboard which provides a skeleton framework of the essential details. The storyboard helps the producer remember the sequence of the story, as films are often shot out of sequence.

Give each child a copy of either photocopiable page 163 or 164, depending upon the ability of the child.

Ask the children to identify the main characters and write these down on the storyboard.

Ask them to decide where the story takes place (the setting) and write this down too.

Ask the class to identify the last episode of the story, then demonstrate how you would write this in brief notes so that a film producer would know what to shoot but not have to read very much of the story.

Ask the group to select either the main complication or the three main episodes that occurred in the story (the opening, the complication and the conclusion). Ask them to write these briefly into the storyboard outline in the correct sequential order and to edit or adapt the conclusion, using your example for guidance.

Discuss with the children whether a film producer would now have a clear idea of the order of the story and the main events that he would need to show in the film version.

3. Story maps

Age range
Six to twelve.

Group size
Pairs.

What you need
Copies of photocopiable page 165, a story involving a journey, pencils, paper, felt-tipped pens, crayons.

What to do
Distribute copies of photocopiable page 165 and discuss how the story of Little Red Riding Hood can be told in pictures. Ask the children to fill in the blank boxes as captions to the pictures.

Read the children the story about a journey, then ask them to work in pairs to draw their own story map.

Ask them to start by deciding what episodes should be included on the map. Let them either illustrate these or precis the events into a box.

When they have finished ask them to give their story maps to another pair to see if they can reconstruct the story from the map.

4. Diary entries

Age range
Any age.

Group size
Whole class working individually or in pairs.

What you need
A story with clearly defined episodes, paper, pens.

What to do
Read the children a story which has some clearly defined episodes, for example, *The Turbulent Term of Tyke Tiler* by Gene Kemp.

Ask the children to work alone or in pairs and to select five different events from the story. Then encourage them to discuss how they would have felt if they had been there.

Ask them to write five diary entries imagining they are a child in the story. Remind them that this is not a retelling of the event but a description of how they would have felt.

When they have finished, let them share their diaries with the rest of the group or class.

5. School report

Age range
Six to twelve.

Group size
Whole class.

What you need
A story with clear portrayal of characters, copies of photocopiable page 166, paper, ruler, pens, pencils.

What to do
Read the children a story with some clear characters portrayed.

Distribute copies of photocopiable page 166. Ask the children to select one of the characters from the story and write a 'school report' for him or her, using the photocopiable sheet. Alternatively, let them devise their own subjects and make their own report sheets.

These could later be displayed with the book in the book corner.

6. Open-ended questions

Age range
Any age.

Group size
Individuals.

What you need
No special equipment.

What to do
Select one or two of the questions below to ask a child when they either finish reading a story to you or tell you that they have finished a book.
• How would you feel if...?
• What would you do today if...?
• What if... had not...?
• Have you ever felt like...?
• Which character did you identify with most strongly?
• What might have happened if...?
• Do you know anyone in real life like...?
• Have you read any other stories with...?
• When did you guess the ending?
• Who do you think would like to read this story?

These questions will help the children to respond to stories more deeply. They could also be used with groups of children to start up discussions.

7. Sound effects

Age range
Any age.

Group size
Whole class.

What you need
A short story, whiteboard, pen, a tape recorder, a range of musical instruments appropriate to the story chosen.

What to do
Read a short story to the class. Ask the children to think what sound effects could be supplied to make the story come more alive. Discuss with the children how they could make these sound effects.

Some sounds might need a few children so different groups could be responsible for the different sound effects.

Write the suggestions on the board and go through the sequence of 'story and sound' with the class.

Read the story again to the class. This time raise your hand when you want them to supply the appropriate sound effect. Lower your hand when you want this to cease.

After a practice, tell the group that they are going to be recorded in action.

Reread the story, signing for sound effects as before, and tape the production. If the group is satisfied with the recording, let them play it to another class.

Variations
The children could be set the challenge of making the sound effects using only their hands or feet, for example, snapping their fingers, rubbing their hands together, drumming their feet.

Small groups could be allowed to select their own short story or write a story which includes many references to 'sounds'. They could use the traditional 'I went on a bear hunt down the path, through the gate, across the river, through the mud, etc' as a model, but with a different scenario, such as 'I went down the school corridor...'.

CHAPTER 13

Comprehension

One of the interesting things about teaching reading is that the notion of comprehension as a task separate from reading usually only rears its head when teaching children aged seven or over. This is quite surprising as genuine reading must have required comprehension from its earliest stages. What seems to happen is that when children reach the age of seven, teachers seek to test specifically the extent to which they have understood what they have read. Traditionally this assessment of a child's skill in comprehending written matter is achieved by using formal comprehension passages, ie. extracts of prose followed by questions which were specifically selected with the intention of testing a child's understanding of a passage.

BACKGROUND

What is wrong with comprehension exercises?

Comprehension tasks are often carried out entirely separately from any other learning. They are not often based upon any ongoing enquiry that the class is undertaking and thus tend to exist in a vacuum.

Children are not expected to bring their own interpretations to bear when answering the questions – that is going beyond the brief of the exercise. For example, a child who answered a question and then 'digressed' into including anecdotal information about his own knowledge of this experience would not be answering 'properly'. It is true that some of the more enlightened publishers of comprehension exercises do include a token open-ended question at the end ('How would you feel if...?') but these are generally considered less valuable in determining the quality of a child's response than the accurate matching of questions to answers embedded in the passage.

The passages chosen are deliberately not based upon children's usual experience with the intention of ensuring that no children will have an unfair advantage over their peers. Consequently the passages are often dull and boring, with titles like 'Georgian and Regency Houses'.

It is also a misnomer to call them 'comprehension exercises'. The child is not intended to read, comprehend, interpret and then take that newly acquired knowledge elsewhere either to share with peers or to inform an ongoing topic. Instead the tasks are isolated from other learning experiences.

Indeed, there is no evidence that children are able to generalise from concepts apparently mastered in comprehension exercises. Children do not automatically transfer the skills used during these exercises to other situations.

Where did many of the slaves in Ancient Greece come from?

Some teachers believe that comprehension exercises provide children with opportunities for close and careful reading in order to answer questions. However, careful observation reveals that many children read the question first and then skim over the passage to find the answer. Because the exercise rarely goes beyond the individual written task, there is no incentive for children to gain deeper understanding. The objective of the exercise is not to increase the child's understanding about anything, merely to answer the questions correctly.

There is plenty of evidence that children learn as much through talking and listening as they do through reading and writing but comprehension exercises are not usually accompanied by discussion where real learning often takes place.

Many comprehension exercises test knowledge only at the literal level. Undoubtedly this is because it is much easier to grade a pupil's work on a right/wrong basis. However, real understanding involves comprehension of both the literal and the inferential. Comprehension exercises do not even assess literal comprehension very successfully. Children *do* need to analyse texts and to recognise the function of various sentences in the structure of the paragraph in order to understand the theme. Unfortunately, comprehension questions do not test any of these skills.

If the weekly comprehension passage does not provide children with the experience of close-study reading, what can you do to give children a real opportunity of this experience?
• Use comprehension passages to encourage children to discuss their understanding of the topic in the light of their own experience.
• Use a passage from an information book on a theme the class is currently exploring.
• Ask 'comprehension type' questions on a passage from a book being read aloud to the class. The pupils will be able to respond with the background knowledge of the rest of the novel.

If comprehension passages, punctuation exercises and general workbook type activities form the bulk of the writing done by children in Y3 to Y6, then they are receiving some misleading messages about writing.
• Writing is regurgitating facts.
• Writing is impersonal and mechanical.
• Questions have answers which are either right or wrong.
• In school one writes inane answers to irrelevant questions.

It is quite possible to read a comprehension passage and then answer questions on it without understanding the passage at all. The following passage reveals just that:

'Last dring there was a chom. The chom flaed for nat chabs. Next gomp all the wuntid were bloved. The wuntid mantered sarily in the pell.'

Questions:

1. When was the chom?
2. What did the chom do?
3. What happened to the wuntid?
4. What did the wuntid do?
5. Would you have enjoyed this experience?

Readers are able to provide 'answers' to the questions simply by juggling with the syntax of the passage. The only question that presents any difficulty is the last one which requires readers to make sense of what has been read and to interpret it in the light of their own experience.

As children move through the junior school, teachers hope that they will develop their reading skills. Key Stage 2 of the National Curriculum sets high standards for pupils, expecting them to become accurate interpreters of texts. They are expected both to understand the literal meaning of a text and to comprehend the underlying ideas. They are also expected to *use* their reading to engage with the rest of the curriculum. It is therefore tempting to employ exercises which purport to encourage children to read and comprehend. However, research has shown that reading comprehension is not made up of a set of discrete subskills. The key to reading comprehension is the single aptitude: the pupils' ability and willingness to *reflect* on whatever they are reading (Lunzer & Gardner, 1979).

We do indeed need to encourage children to reflect as they read, but traditional comprehension exercises do not encourage real reflection.

In busy classrooms with large classes it might be perfectly reasonable to use set comprehension exercises for some children to do while you are occupied with another group of children. It is often part of good classroom management to have tasks which some children can complete without assistance from you. However, it is important to realise that while those children are indeed being kept busy, the chances of much real learning taking place are slim.

The following activities suggest alternative ways in which to encourage children to read with purpose, to be selective with information in a text and genuinely to 'comprehend' its meaning.

ACTIVITIES

1. Follow the instructions

Age range
Seven to twelve.

Group size
Pairs.

What you need
Instructions and appropriate materials for making simple paper or cardboard items such as a thaumatrope, a spinner or a turning wheel. (Often good ideas for these are given in activity books or children's magazines.)

What to do
Although children are frequently asked to follow instructions in the classroom, very often these instructions are read out or produced by the teacher. This activity will demonstrate how they interpret instructions for themselves.

Ask each pair to read the instructions and work together to make the item.

When the children have finished, discuss the items and the instructions for making them. Did the children find the instructions sufficiently clear?

2. Follow the directions

Age range
Seven to twelve.

Group size
Pairs.

What you need
Road maps (It is often better to use maps printed in book form as large folding maps are rather unmanageable in the classroom.), pencils, paper.

What to do
Set pairs of children the task of finding a route between two specified points on the map. Explain that they will need to make notes about their chosen route.

This activity can be self-checking, as once the route has been identified pairs can swap routes. Other pairs can then work from the notes to find the destination on the map.

3. Open-ended questions

Age range
Seven to twelve.

Group size
Any size.

What you need
Passages set for comprehension.

What to do
Either read the passage to the group while they follow the text or ask individuals to read it to a partner. Once the passage has been read, ignore the printed questions and ask open-ended questions about the passage, for example:
• What part of the passage did you like best?
• How did you feel when...?
• Did you expect that....?
• What clues did you have to help you expect that?

   All of these questions require a close reading of the text in order to answer them, but they also require reflection and internalisation of the text that is often missing from standard comprehension exercises.

4. Cloze

Age range
Seven to twelve.

Group size
Pairs.

What you need
Pencils, copies of a passage, either from a work of fiction or from a non-fiction text related to the topic the children are currently exploring, with some words deleted. These deletions can be made according to different reasons for setting the particular passage. For example:
• Key nouns could be deleted from a passage on a topic where the children have become familiar with the relevant vocabulary;
• Every tenth word could be deleted;
• All adjectives could be deleted;
• A whole line could be deleted. (NB. It is only possible for the children to be able to make sensible suggestions as to the omitted line when it has been preceded by a considerable amount of text.)

What to do
Ask the children to work in pairs to fill in the gaps in the text. This should result in discussion about the likely 'answers' and encourages careful reading, rereading and reflection. Later the children will be interested to learn which words the author used in the passage. These may be the same words that they selected, or the children's alternatives may be just as appropriate. The point about this exercise is that in most instances there is usually more than one good answer.

5. Sequencing poetry

Age range
Seven to twelve.

Group size
Pairs.

What you need
Photocopies of a poem cut into separate lines, envelopes.

What to do
Put the lines of the photocopied poem into envelopes and hand them out to each pair of children. Ask them to try to reconstruct the poem.

   Sometimes there will be only one 'answer' to this activity, but on other occasions there will be perfectly reasonable alternative versions of the poem.

6. Making a poem

Age range
Nine to twelve.

Group size
Pairs.

What you need
Photocopies of a short poem cut up into individual words, envelope, paper, pencils.

What to do
Hand out to each pair an envelope containing the individual words of the poem and ask them to make their own poem from the words. Explain that they can omit up to five of the words if they wish.

When they have finished, make a class book of the poems, asking each pair to write out their version of the poem. Let them refer to the original poem to see how their poem differs from it.

7. Emotions and feelings

Age range
Nine to twelve.

Group size
Pairs.

What you need
Some well-known stories, paper, pencils.

What to do
Either read aloud some well-known tales, such as Goldilocks, or check on the children's knowledge of the story by talking about it.

Ask each pair to write a list of feelings or emotions expressed by a character. This activity works best if you introduce it, giving the children a model to follow. For example, Goldilocks was:
- *bold* to enter the cottage;
- *tempted* to try the porridge;
- *cheeky* to go upstairs;
- *careless* to fall asleep.

Ask the children to identify the feelings or emotions and justify their inclusion in the list.

Once children have done this activity on several well-known tales, they will enjoy doing it on new stories read in group reading sessions or on a story read aloud by you.

8. Ask a question – 1

Age range
Nine to twelve.

Group size
Five or six children.

What you need
A story, pieces of card, pens.

What to do
After the children have shared a story, either in a group reading session or after a class read-aloud, ask each child to write a question about the story on to a piece of card. Remind the children of the techniques of good questioning. Point out to them that questions which require only factual recall to provide the answer are boring questions and will elicit boring answers.

Shuffle the questions together, then let one child draw a card and try to answer the question. Ask the person who made up the question to decide if the answer given fully answers the question. If it does not, ask the question-poser to add the details that she thinks are missing from the answer which has been given.

This activity works also with non-fiction. Remind the children of the techniques of good questioning – questions which require only factual recall to provide the answer are boring questions and will elicit boring answers!

9. Ask a question – 2

Age range
Nine to twelve.

Group size
Pairs.

What you need
Passages set for comprehension, overhead projector, pens.

What to do
Ask the children to work with a partner, first reading the passage then deciding what questions they could ask about it. This is another activity which works best if you model it first for all the class, perhaps by using an overhead projector to display the passage for everyone to see and then by negotiating some good questions to ask about the passage.

The children will need guidance to avoid asking questions which only require a factual knowledge of the text. They will soon realise that this results in identical answers which are not very interesting.

You can then suggest ways to interpret the text on a more personal level, by asking questions which require a more considered response. This activity has a self-checking element as one pair of children could pass on both their passage and their questions for another pair to answer.

10. Character matrix

Age range
Eight to twelve.

Group size
Pairs.

What you need
Copies of photocopiable page 167, pencils.

What to do
After the children have had a group reading session or after a class read-aloud, give them copies of photocopiable page 167 and invite them to complete the character matrix.

Explain that they need to decide which characters they intend to analyse in this way and then fill in the matrix. It is important that children also explain *why* they have made certain judgements about certain characters.

As a development of this activity it can be quite interesting for children to complete a character matrix when only halfway through a story. They can then make another matrix at the end of the story and compare the results. This might reveal some of the techniques the author has used when presenting a character and it might discourage children from making hasty character assessments based on incomplete or misleading information.

CHAPTER 14

The bilingual reader

When English is a second language for children in Y3 and above, they tend to try to acquire the language rapidly. They generally have a good command of their own language, have subconsciously grasped its 'abstract' rules and are on the look out for short cuts into English. They have learned to interpret a speaker's gestures, body language, expression, even tones of voice, and they mimic this learning when answering questions.

This can give the impression of a fluency in English that is misleading to the busy teacher and frequently results in the teacher over-estimating the child's knowledge. This may

be compounded by the child apparently being able to read in English with intonation and expression. If he has already learned to read in his own language and in his own script, this knowledge of what it sounds like is transferred to the production of English words. The child has learned to 'crack the code' of the words and therefore reads with apparent understanding. We can appreciate this as adults when we visit a country whose language we do not know, particularly a phonetically regular language such as Spanish or Italian. Very quickly we can

'read' the billboards and the newspaper headings with a passable accent, yet have very little understanding of what we are reading.

The use of a different script can momentarily delay this kind of 'fluency' but it is surprising how quickly children absorb the change. However, if they relax their vigilance or become tired, they may revert to the forms of their own language, perhaps reading a word backwards or automatically looking to the right-hand side of the page to start reading.

BACKGROUND

Teachers with children whose first language is not English need to make careful and systematic observations of when and how the children use English. However, it is also essential to gain as much information as possible about each child's background, use and command of his first language.

• What is his first language?
• Do the parents and child use this language exclusively at home?
• Can the child read in this language?

• Do the parents have in the house many books, papers and magazines written in their first language?
• Does the child enjoy being read to in his first language?
• Is the child able to write in his first language?
• What is the main language of his local community?
• Are there other children in the class who can speak his language?
• Does the child attend a Saturday morning community school?
• Does the family observe certain religious festivals?
• Has the family been separated for any length of time, for example during extended trips abroad?

• Does the child require a special diet?
• Where did the child attend school before? Are there any records available from this school?

Unfortunately, most teachers are not bilingual and will obviously experience difficulty in communicating if the child's parents do not speak any English. However, other parents are generally only too willing to help and if they do speak the language they can do an enormous amount to help the child and his family feel more at home in the community.

Having acquired as much background information as possible, you need to set time aside to observe and assess the new bilingual child in the class and to pay careful attention to the way he uses English when talking to others.

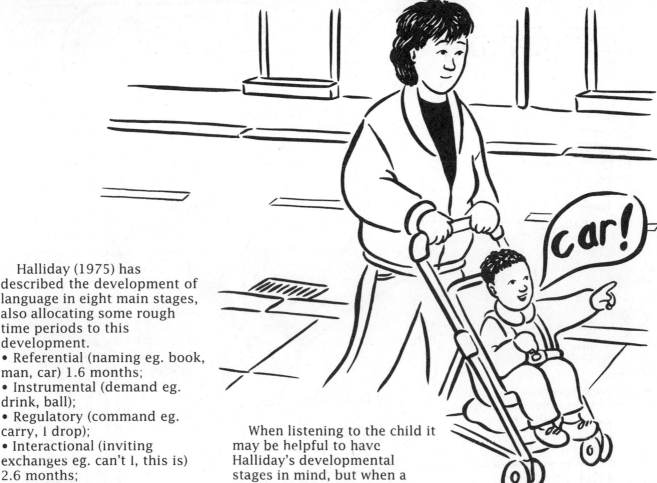

Halliday (1975) has described the development of language in eight main stages, also allocating some rough time periods to this development.
• Referential (naming eg. book, man, car) 1.6 months;
• Instrumental (demand eg. drink, ball);
• Regulatory (command eg. carry, I drop);
• Interactional (inviting exchanges eg. can't I, this is) 2.6 months;
• Personal (eg. I like, I want, more use of pronouns);
• Heuristic (exploring eg. what's this, why, use of possessive) 3.6 months;
• Imaginary (fantasy eg. let's pretend);
• Informative (predicting, empathising eg. can I help).

However, this process reflects acquiring a first language on a one-to-one basis, with a parent constantly attending to the child's needs. This is impossible to replicate for the older second-language learner. He may be immersed in English, but it will be in the company of his peers who hardly see their role as 'language developers' and who are unlikely to feel they need to 'attend to the needs' of one of their group.

When listening to the child it may be helpful to have Halliday's developmental stages in mind, but when a child is learning a language you must remember that the speaker is likely to have a far greater understanding (receptive vocabulary) than spoken (productive) vocabulary.

Listening to a child's spoken 'miscues' can give valuable insight into how the child is manipulating the language. Some 'errors' are obviously due to a direct translation from the mother tongue, others may result from a confusion with pronouns, especially 'he' and 'she'. If these are picked up quickly and the child is given practice and good models, it may avoid these becoming embedded into the child's language. You need to make sure that as much talk as possible is 'situational' so that pointing and demonstration is automatically part of the scenario. By including as much repetition of phrases as possible and by encouraging imitation, the child may quickly absorb some of the rules and patterns of English which he can then apply to a new situation.

You can learn a lot about the child from observation.
• Listen to how the child constructs his sentences.
• Listen to how the child asks questions.
• Observe how much the child relies on body language.
• Listen out for confusion over pronouns, especially 'he' and 'she'.

• Observe how much the child expects others to complete his sentences.

• Note how often the child wants to reread a book. Is this because he is reading it with pleasure and understanding, or is it because it is familiar and he can read it in a way that pleases the teacher and his parents?

• Try to assess the child's ability to listen.

• Beware of using too much metaphor or irony. These are very difficult for second-language learners to understand.

• Encourage the child to produce 'free and unaided' writing for you on a regular basis.

• Observe how the child works in different group situations. If possible try to place him in a group where a peer does speak his language.

• Observe how he plays and participates in playground activities.

• Try to assess how easily he switches between languages and how appropriately he does this.

Remember that moving into another culture is exhausting and also very disorientating. Although you and the school may be eager for the child to absorb this new life and new language quickly, and to feel happy and secure with it, this is more likely to be achieved when the child and the parents feel welcomed and appreciated for the contribution they can make through their own culture and with their own language. The photocopiable sheet on page 168 could be used to display in the entrance hall or around the school. Encouraging children to write in their own language, asking parents to make taped stories in their own language for children to listen to or asking them to come into school to tell stories of their childhood or tales that they know, all contribute to creating a safe and comfortable environment in which the child is more likely to thrive.

The following activities are designed to promote talking. Obviously they can be used with all children, but children for whom English is a second language need even more 'talking time' if they are to develop into readers. For these children, paired work and group discussions need to have priority over other areas of the curriculum.

ACTIVITIES

1. The second-hand artist

Age range
Any age.

Group size
Two to eight children.

What you need
Paper, ruler, pencils, coloured crayons.

What to do
Use a ruler and pencil to divide the paper into six or eight squares. Make sure each member of the group has a sheet of paper.

Select six or eight simple objects for the group to draw. Appoint one member of the group the 'caller' and allow her to tell the rest of the group what to draw in each square, giving careful and clear directions *only once*. For example, 'In the top left hand corner draw a table. In the bottom right hand corner draw a chair,' and so on.

Variation
Ask the group to draw objects but add some positional language. For example, 'In the top left hand corner draw a table. *On* the table draw a book. In the bottom right hand corner draw a chair. *Under* the chair draw a cat.'

NB. The caller should use the same sentence format for each item until she is certain that all the group know this form of direction. She can then change the format. For example, 'Where is the chair? What is under the chair?'

Draw a house with a blue roof

2. Pathways

Age range
Any age.

Group size
Two to eight children.

What you need
A copy of either photocopiable page 169 or 170 for each player. (Page 169 is more suitable for younger players, page 170 for older children.)

What to do
If the group is going to use photocopiable page 170, explain that they are going to give instructions on how to escape from the island.

First, let one child choose which path to start on. Ask him to give clear directions to the others so that they can travel along the same path. For example, 'We shall go down the path between Shark Bay and Coconut Corner' or 'We shall go down the path between Coconut Corner and the Old Swamp.'

When the path divides, let another child choose the route.

When they get to the ship, ask the groups to show each other the routes they have drawn and compare them.

Younger children can use photocopiable page 169 in the same way.

3. Going shopping

Age range
Any age.

Group size
Two to eight children.

What you need
Small pictures of things to buy, such as clothes, pets, food, hobby accessories and presents, cut up and mounted on to card (catalogues from big stores are a useful source for this).

What to do
Explain to the group that they are going 'shopping' and, using the picture cards, they must say what they are going to buy. Explain that they must say exactly the same words each time but that they should add their own choice of shopping item by selecting something else from the pile of cards. For example:

First player: 'I am going to the shops to buy a rabbit.'
(The first player picks up the relevant picture and places it in the centre of the table.)
Second player: 'I am going shopping to buy a rabbit and a hair brush.'
(The second player puts a picture of a hair brush next to the rabbit.)

Continue play in this way until all the pictures have been placed in the row. Then, the next player should say, 'I have been shopping and I bought a rabbit.' She should then remove the card or turn it over.

The following player then says, 'I have been shopping and I bought a rabbit and a hair brush,' and removes the second card. Play continues until all the cards have been removed.

Any player who is unable to remember the sequence is 'out'.

If this proves difficult, ask the players to work in pairs and encourage them to help each other to remember the sequence.

Variations
• The players play without cards and have to try to remember what the previous players have put on the list. Ensure that all the players know the vocabulary of the objects chosen.
• The players have to select items in alphabetical order. It is useful to have an alphabet strip card placed on the table for the players to see. As the players become more familiar with this game they can increase the difficulty by adding adjectives to the

objects. For example, 'I went shopping and I bought an adventurous ant.' 'I went shopping and I bought an adventurous ant and a beastly bear.'

4. Did you hear that?

Age range
Any age.

Group size
Whole class, later working in pairs.

What you need
Pencils, paper, copies of a story, a second version of the story with deliberate errors included, for example:
• a whole word wrong: Goldilocks walked along the winding *roof*;
• the initial sound wrong: Goldilocks walked along the winding *bath*;
• the punctuation wrong: Goldilocks walked. Along the winding path;
• the fact wrong: The butterfly lays its eggs in a nest.

What to do
Give each player a copy of the correct text. Read the incorrect passage to the group and ask them to mark every time you read something that is incorrect, for example, by circling the word.

At the end of the passage, go through it with the children and discuss the 'errors' with them, using comments such as, 'Did anyone circle anything in this line? Well done! I misread "cat".'

Alternatively read the passage to the group and ask them to identify orally anything that is wrong as you read.

Develop this further by asking the group to work in pairs to make their own 'deliberate errors' for the rest of the class. Either give them a passage from a book on which to work or allow them to make up their own text and create their own alterations.

5. Spot the sound

Age range
Any age.

Group size
Any size.

What you need
A passage of text with either a large number of words starting with the same sound or with rhymes, paper, pencil. (Simple poems, alphabet alliteration sentences are useful starters for this.)

What to do
Tell the group that they have to listen to your 'story' and every time they hear a word starting with a certain letter or rhyming with a certain word they are to make a mark on their sheet of paper.

When you have finished reading, check the children's answers.

As the children become adept at this, increase the difficulty by adding more sounds for them to identify.

Finally, let the group write their own 'Spot the sound' passages, choosing a sound or rhyme for the others to

It's small and round and soft

identify. Again they could do this by using a published poem or passage.

6. What have I got?

Age range
Any age.

Group size
Two to six children.

What you need
A large soft bag, a selection of small objects (eg. pencil, soft toy, book, cup, paint brush).

What to do
Put the objects into the bag and let the children take it in turns to put in their hands and describe what they can feel. Encourage them to say at least

three things about it. After each turn, ask the others in the group to say what they think the object is, using the child's comments as clues. Ask the child who put her hand into the bag to say what she thinks the object is.

Finally, bring the object out of the box so that the children can identify it.

7. What am I thinking about?

Age range
Any age.

Group size
Small groups or whole class.

What you need
No special requirements.

What to do
Ask one of the children to think of an object, person, or place. Ask him to tell the group which category he has chosen, plus two pieces of information as clues. For example, 'It is a

person in a story. She is female.'

Let the group ask questions about this person, but tell them that they can only have three guesses as to the final name.

Variations
Limit the number of questions the group can ask, for example, twenty questions only before a final guess must be made.

You can also limit the number of questions that receive the answer 'no', for example, only five. This will increase the difficulty of the game and thus its successful use will depend on the players' command of English.

8. Where am I going?

Age range
Any age.

Group size
Pairs to whole class.

What you need
No special requirements.

What to do
Select a place in the school, for example, the staffroom, the

dining room, or the library. Without letting the children know which place you have chosen, describe the route you would have to take to get there.

Ask the children to decide where you are by trying to follow the directions in their minds.

When they are used to this, let the children try to select and describe a place to get to.

A similar game could be 'What am I making or doing?' Describe an activity, such as painting a picture, marking the register or eating sandwiches, and ask the class to guess what the activity is.

9. Spot the difference

Age range
Any age.

Group size
Individuals or pairs.

What you need
Copies of photocopiable page 171 (for younger children) or page 172 (for older children).

What to do
Distribute copies of photocopiable page 171 or 172, depending upon the age of the children. Ask the children to work individually or in pairs to describe the differences between the two pictures.

Do not let the children mark the pictures. The object is to encourage vocabulary development.

10. What's wrong?

Age range
Any age.

Group size
Individuals or pairs.

What you need
Copies of photocopiable page 173.

What to do
Distribute copies of photocopiable page 173. Ask the children to describe what is wrong. Explain that they may not mark the pictures.

11. Tell the story

Age range
Any age.

Group size
Two to four children.

What you need
Two copies of a picture book or copies of photocopiable page 174, scissors, card, adhesive.

I go down the corridor, through the double doors,....

What to do

Mount picture sequences from the book, leaving out the text. Alternatively, cut up a copy of photocopiable page 174 and mount the pictures on to card. Give the pictures to the group and ask them to create a text to tell the 'story' or directions to match the cards. They can either tell this to the class or they can write captions for the pictures and display them as appropriate. If a picture book is being used, remember that the order should be dictated by the story the children create.

Some useful books to use are:

Brown, Ruth *The World That Jack Built*, Andersen Press (1990).
Burningham, John *Mr Gumpy's Motor Car*, Picture Puffin (1979).
Gretz, Susanna *The Bears Who Stayed Indoors*, Picture Puffin (1987).

Hutchins, Pat *You'll Soon Grow into Them, Titch*, Picture Puffin (1983).
Hutchins, Pat *Rosie's Walk*, Picture Puffin (1970).
Marshall, Edward *Fox at School*, Bodley Head (1984).
Traditional Tales series, published by Ladybird.

Some stories from the early stages in scheme books and information books that are illustrated with photographs are also a reasonable source for this activity. For example, 'Sunshine' from Heinemann, 'Story Chest' from Nelson, 'Literacy Links' from Kingcourt, 'My World' (simple information) from Nelson, and 'Bookshelf' (stories and information) from Harcourt, Brace, Jovanovitch.

12. What happens next?

Age range
Any age.

Group size
Whole class.

What you need
A selection of short stories.

What to do
Read the beginning of the story to the children and stop at a 'cliff-hanger'. Ask the group to predict what will happen next.

Chi had never been to the seaside before.....

Ensure that they use the clues they have been given in the text so that they do not make wild predictions.

Read on until you either confirm or change their opinions. Ask them to predict again and then continue to read on.

This activity helps children to realise that reading involves responding to and understanding the text, not just sounding the words.

Variations

Start a story as above and ask a child to predict the next episode. Then ask the next child in the group to decide what will happen after that. Build up this story, if possible writing it down for the group, and offer possible solutions if the children begin to struggle. Finally, compare the story they have created with the version in the original book.

Let the children write out and illustrate their story and display it alongside the published version.

13. Missing manuscript

Age range
Any age.

Group size
Individuals or pairs.

What you need
A collection of postcards or photographs, paper, pencils, tape recorder.

What to do
Give each child or pair of children one or two of the pictures to look at. Tell the children that the card or cards you have given them is all that is left from a precious manuscript. Ask them to tell the story that this must have illustrated.

Let them choose whether to write this down, record their ideas on to tape or tell the rest of the class their version.

14. Watch the space

Age range
Any age.

Group size
Pairs.

What you need
Copies of photocopiable pages 175 and 176 or a passage of text from which a number of words have been deleted (the deletions can be one word, one phrase or a whole sentence. Remember that more text is needed in between if the deletion is more than one word. The word deletion could be on a regular basis, such as every twelfth word, or it could be all the adjectives, verbs, adverbs or conjunctions), pencils.

What to do
Give a copy of the text to each child. Ask the children to read the text in pairs and to try to work out which words would fit correctly into the spaces. Encourage them to do this orally first then, when they have agreed as to the best replacement, let them write in the missing words.

Encourage the children to compare their answers with

other pairs when they have finished. Finally, share all the possible answers with the class, discussing the sense and value of each suggestions.

15. Judge for yourself

Age range
Any age.

Group size
Two to six children.

What you need
A simple version of a traditional tale.

What to do
Ask the group to read the tale together, either by one member of the group reading to the others, or by taking it in turns to read aloud.

When they have finished reading, ask the group to retell the story. It is essential that they should have a clear idea of the events and the order in which they occur.

Ask the group to select a character in the story and to retell the events from this new point of view. For example, they could retell the giant's story in 'Jack and the Beanstalk', the wolf's story in 'Red Riding Hood', the prince's story in 'Cinderella', or the step-mother's story in 'Sleeping Beauty'. Let them dramatise their version, write it out and display it or tell it to the rest of the class.

Ask the class to judge which is the strongest story, the traditional point of view or the new interpretation.

16. Idiomatic match

Age range
Any age.

Group size
Two to four children.

What you need
Copies of photocopiable pages 177 and 178, scissors, card, adhesive.

What to do
Stick a copy of photocopiable page 177 on to a piece of card and cut along the dotted lines.

Put all the strips of card face-up on to the table and ask the children to take turns to choose an expression and to find its matching strip. If they succeed, let them keep the two matching strips. The winner is the player with the most pairs.

Variations
Write sentences containing metaphors or similes on to cards and ask the children to match metaphors with their meanings. Encourage the children to explain why they have chosen to put two strips together.

This could also be extended to proverbs and their meanings (see photocopiable page 178).

CHAPTER 15

The struggling reader

Every child in a primary classroom is, at some time, going to be confronted with text that she finds difficult to read. This may be because the reader is meeting a new subject or because the sentence is complex and the associated terminology is unfamiliar, but most of the time children can expect to be given books that they find manageable and interesting. However, there is also a number of children for whom all reading and writing is an enormous effort. Teachers often agonise as to how to help them acquire the necessary skills so that they too can experience reading as a pleasure, for information and enjoyment.

BACKGROUND

Why don't all children learn to read?

Failure to learn to read can be attributed to many causes – some are physical, some emotional, some social and some cultural, but although research has been extensive the causes seem as diverse as the children and no one method or explanation is the answer.

Who are the strugglers?

Some children who are struggling with reading are easy to identify. They obviously have great difficulty in decoding print. They read pedantically, word by word, constantly demanding either the teacher's attention or that of their peers, and having

produced this 'sound to the print' they then seem unable to retain any of the information. These children obviously need specialised help and many schools do provide this as often as possible. These 'readers' still need the experiences that children receive on first coming to school, but adapted to their interests and age. There is no short cut to acquiring reading and if the 'sure-fire-quick method' is applied, children are often left insecure and on even more shaky foundations. (Suggestions for helping these children can be found in *Inspirations for Becoming a Reader*, D. Bentley et al (1992), Scholastic Publications Ltd.)

However, some of the more independent readers also struggle. These children, when pushed, can read the words but appear to derive no

pleasure or understanding from them. They are more difficult to identify for they demonstrate reader-like behaviour which disguises their inability to respond to what they read. These 'independent' readers, too, need constant observation and encouragement.

Children manifest their insecurity in many different ways – some become quiet and withdrawn, and remarkably adept at fading into the background, others become neat and careful copiers to overshadow their problems, while others are noisy and disruptive, trying to attract the admiration and attention of their friends by this behaviour.

All these children have a very low self-image and genuinely believe that they will never succeed at reading.

'Even when you're getting better you never catch up 'cos the others are getting better an' all so you're still as far behind.' Tracy, aged ten.

'Sometimes I think it might be better not to read than go on and on at something that's dead hard. I'm not daft but I feel like a little kid showing the teacher what I can't do.' Keith, aged nine and a half.

'Me dad can't read and he says its his fault. I cannot and me mam tries and helps us but she couldn't read – not 'til she was a woman and I'll never be one of them!' Stephen, aged nine. (Quotations taken from 'Why Can't I Read', *Reading Journal* (1986) 20,1.)

The role of the teacher

You may not know exactly why a child is struggling with reading but you still have to help that child to become a reader to the best of his ability. However, before launching into any programme or method, it is essential to establish what the child already knows and when the child's problems began. It is also important to create a supportive and friendly environment in which the child's efforts receive constant and genuine praise.

Changing the child's attitude to reading

Children who have begun to realise that they are not 'keeping up' with their peers also begin to believe that it is because they *cannot* do it. The first step is to persuade these children they will succeed and to show them why they need to learn to read. This is not a quick or easy achievement, but spending time observing what they can do and constantly telling them where they are successful goes a long way to boosting their confidence.

Characteristics of the child with reading difficulties

Children who feel they are failing quickly begin to use avoidance strategies in order to cover up their inadequacies. These children do not willingly choose to read or comment upon a book. They ask to do other activities, such as tidying up an area of the classroom, going on an errand or copying out some work in best, which they know will win the approval of the busy teacher. They rarely know the title of a book or an author and, in class discussion, will wait until others have offered suggestions before repeating this information as though it was their own. For example, they too will claim that Roald Dahl is their favourite author! They rarely borrow a book from the library or book corner unless they have been directed to do so. However, some older children have also learned that this behaviour wins approval and may indeed frequently register that they have taken out a book. The question is, have they read it?

It may be possible to identify the struggling child by the way she reads aloud and especially by the retelling of the text, but hesitancy and a lack of fluency is not the prerogative of a poor reader. It can also be a characteristic of the child who is responding to the text and processing the information as she reads (see Chapter 12, 'Hearing children read').

Establishing a programme

A good starting point is to find out what the child already knows and build on it. It is essential to make a record of strengths and weaknesses, and useful to consider attitudes and skills (see photocopiable pages 179 and 180).

The next task is to try to set a realistic goal that the child can achieve. This may be to encourage the child to follow a text of a recorded story or to discuss with a child a story that he has just been told. It may be to teach a basic concept about print that he seemed unsure of or it may be to speed up the reading of a text that he could cope with but with which he has been over-hesitant.

Obviously it is essential to find material that interests and engages the child while at the same time not insulting him with its simpler content and layout. This is not easy to find and the small amount of published material available is woefully inadequate. It is important that the child genuinely wants to read the text and is supported in that aim. You might like to use a magazine or book that is about a hobby the child enjoys. Indeed, the text may be difficult but you can read it to the child, write out comments and information that the child offers and use this material for highlighting his skills, vocabulary and reason for reading.

Whenever a task is completed you need to evaluate that task, discussing with the child what he has achieved and where he can go next. It can be valuable to keep a sheet with the strengths and weaknesses clearly recorded (Figure 1). This can be used for later discussion with the child and the parent. Remember that the struggling reader needs *proof* that he is improving. It is only by constantly setting realistic goals, and by showing him how and what he has achieved, that the child will believe that he can become a reader.

Below are some descriptions of the most common characteristics of the struggling reader. The solutions suggested are brief and may not cover the needs of all children. However, the points raised can be considered and you can add to them as appropriate.

Child uninterested in reading

• Find out if there are any hobbies or clubs that interest the child. Help her to choose magazines or books that contain information about her interest. If necessary, record some of the articles on tape for the child to follow.
• Help the child to write and talk about her interest and present this to the class. Ensure that the child is recognised as an 'expert' to raise her self-esteem.
• Allow the child time to browse among 'non-threatening' books, such as picture books or fully illustrated information books. Try to ensure that the child begins to see the value of books and reading.
• Provide videos of the books the child reads. This also allows the child to 'know' and comment upon books her peers are reading.
• Provide short stories recorded on tape that reflect her interests and that are at the right level.

Hesitant and stumbling read

• Provide material that the child can read easily. Encourage him to read on to

Name:	Angela H.		
Date	Strengths	Weaknesses	Where next
3rd March	Read for more fluently. Well done!	Try to remember to miss out the problem words and read on. Don't wait for me to tell you!	Try to do some 'cloze' sheets with your friend.

Figure 1

tape so that he can listen to the way he reads.
• Ask the child to help younger children who are just beginning to read. Let him either read to the infants or prepare taped versions of books for them.
• Provide well-read versions of interesting/exciting stories on tape for him to follow.
• Ask him to run his finger under the text as you read to him. Then encourage him to try to read the text at that pace for himself. Choose short passages for this activity.
• Encourage him to take part in group reading and play reading (see Chapter 7, 'Group reading').
• Encourage the child to leave out a difficult word and read on. Some children like to substitute the word 'something' when they meet an unknown word.
• Provide opportunities for simultaneous paired reading with a friend or partner.
• Make a note of the words that cause a problem and help the child to learn to write them.

Reads without understanding
• Read the book to him and talk about the story. Check he can understand when it is read aloud.
• Read small sections with the child and then stop and recall what has been read.
• Initially ask the child for factual recall of the text and praise this literal knowledge. When the child is confident with this, ask questions that promote understanding and response.
• Encourage the child to draw story maps with you or devise reading board games, wordsearches and so on, that use the places and characters in the book.
• Encourage the child to do as much oral retelling of texts as possible. Remember this should include both fiction and non-fiction.
• Encourage the child to predict what will happen both in stories you are reading to the group and in the books he is reading.

Some books to entice the reluctant reader

Fiction
Funnybones J. & A. Ahlberg, 1980 (Little Mammoth).
Animalia G. Base, 1986 (Macmillan).
Piggy Book A. Browne, 1986 (Julia MacRae).
The Planet of Terror P. Burston, 1985 (Walker Books).
The Slimy Book B. Cole, 1985 (Jonathan Cape).
Where's Wally? M. Handford, 1987 (Walker Books).
Pirates C. & J. Hawkins, 1987 (Collins).
The Great Green Mouse Disaster M. Waddell, 1981 (Andersen Press).
Dr Xargle's Book of Earth Hounds J. Willis, 1989 (Andersen Press).

Non-fiction
Amazing Worlds A. Parsons, 1990 (Dorling Kindersley)
Look at... books R. Thornson, 1989 (Franklyn Watts).
New World (green level) C. Butterworth, 1988 (Nelson).
Sunshine non-fiction (early levels) J. Gilbert, 1989 (Heinemann).
Lemons (level 2) G. Davies, 1988 (Blackwell).
Usborne Starting Points K. Woodward, 1991 (Usborne).
Usborne Conservation Guides K. Khanduri, 1991 (Usborne).

ACTIVITIES

1. Would you rather?

Age range
Any age.

Group size
Pairs or small groups.

What you need
Books for the children to read.

What to do
Devise questions linked to the text the children are reading. These questions should be in the form of choices, for example, 'Would you rather be Little Red Riding Hood's grandmother or the wolf?' Ask the group to choose which alternative they would prefer and to say why.

Explain that it is not enough just to select a character, they also have to justify their choice.

Once the children become used to this let them suggest alternative choices and offer these to the class for discussion.

2. What do you think happens now?

Age range
Any age.

Group size
Four to six children.

What you need
Enough copies of a story for the children to have one each, card, pen, scissors, pencil, paper.

What to do
Cut the card into strips and write 'What do you think happens now?' on each one. At strategic intervals place the strips of card into each copy of the book.

Give each member of the group a copy of the book and ask them to start reading together. When they reach the pieces of card, ask the children to stop and try to predict what will happen next. One of the children can act as scribe and make notes on what the group think.

On finishing the story, ask the children to compare their predictions with the original.

there are in the world?' she might suggest three possible answers: two, three or five.

Finally, the 'expert' should reveal the correct information (which, in the above example, is three).

5. True or false?

Age range
Any age.

Group size
Whole class.

What you need
A simple encyclopaedia or non-fiction books (Usborne information books are excellent for this kind of information as they include some astonishing facts. See list of suggested books for the struggling reader on page 137.), paper, pencil.

What to do
Ask the children to find out as many 'facts' as possible on a chosen topic and to write them down. Then ask them to devise some false 'facts' and intersperse them among the correct information.

Let the children take turns to ask the class which facts they think are true and which are false.

Finally let the children reveal the 'true' information.

another group. Encourage them to discuss which they think is the best choice in each case.

4. Mastermind

Age range
Any age.

Group size
Whole class.

What you need
A copy of photocopiable page 182, a simple encyclopaedia or relevant non-fiction books.

What to do
Ask one child to be the 'expert', and to choose a subject and find out three main facts about it. Explain that she should then think of two other possibilities which may sound likely to the non-expert and write these on to a copy of photocopiable page 182.

Let the 'expert' ask the other children in the class to guess which are the correct facts. For example, if the 'expert' asked 'How many kinds of rhinoceroses do you think

3. Cloze that space

Age range
Any age.

Group size
Individuals or groups of up to four children.

What you need
Either a copy of the texts on page 181 or a passage from which you have deleted selected words.

What to do
Ask the child or group to try to replace the missing words on photocopiable page 181. Explain that there is no one correct answer, but that they must put in words that make sense.

Let the children compare their choice of words with

6. Find the order

Age range
Any age.

Group size
Two to six children.

What you need
Card, pen, scissors.

What to do
Write the main events of a well-known story on pieces of card. Cut up the story either into separate sentences or into paragraphs and give the children the shuffled text. Ask them to try to decide what sequence the text should follow.

Ask them to read you their final choice.

Show them the author's order and discuss with them any changes they made.

Variations
This can be done with pictures alone, text alone or pictures and text.

The children might like to try to write their own story and put this on to card. They could then cut this into strips for you to re-sequence!

7. Wordsearch

Age range
Any age.

Group size
Pairs.

What you need
A copy of photocopiable page 183, a story with several characters and places mentioned in it, pencils.

What to do
Read the children a story, then ask them to work in pairs to use photocopiable page 183 to devise a wordsearch associated with the story they have just read. Remind them that the words can go vertically, horizontally and diagonally. Encourage them to make sure they are spelling the words correctly by checking against the book. Place this wordsearch into the back of the book for future readers to try to complete.

8. Write a review

Age range
Any age.

Group size
Pairs/whole class.

What you need
Copies of photocopiable page 184, pencils.

What to do
Read photocopiable page 184 to the children and discuss with them the various categories into which the books fall. Ask them to choose a book they have read recently and to fill in a copy of the sheet accordingly.

Ask for volunteers to tell the story of their book and to explain how they have marked the review sheet.

Collect the reviews and display them in the book corner for other potential readers to consult.

CHAPTER 16

Parents: an ongoing partnership

Many parents take an active interest when their child begins to learn to read. Indeed, sometimes it seems to become an almost excessive anxiety as parents worry if their child will succeed. As the vast majority of children become happy and successful readers in their own good time, so parental interest in their child's progress declines. Once a child has entered the junior school parental interest is often barely noticeable. However, parents do play a part in their child's development as an independent reader and it is important to encourage them in that role.

BACKGROUND

Obsessive interest in the early acquisition of reading can hinder progress. Children can become so anxious and fearful of disappointing their parents that they seize up when faced with a book to read. Teachers of children in the early years have to work hard to channel parents' interest into more beneficial means of support, while teachers of children aged seven to twelve often have an uphill task persuading parents to show any interest at all! The same parents who were distraught if their five-year-old could read the word 'the' one day and not the next, are quite happy to be ignorant about which books their eight-year-old may have read over the past four weeks, and indeed ignorant as to whether she has read any books at all in the past month!

It is important to try to get parents to relax in the early stages but to take an active interest later in their child's developing reading skills.

Once children have mastered initial reading skills they still need continual support and encouragement to maintain an interest in reading. The responsibility for this role, a role which Aidan Chambers (1991) calls 'the enabling adult', is best shared between the teacher and the home.

What can parents do to help?

• They can be encouraged to show an interest in what their child is reading. This may take the form of hearing their child read, or asking the child about what he has read.
• They can be encouraged to show their children how reading is an important part of life by letting the children see them reading newspapers, telephone directories, maps, Teletext, recipe books, bus timetables, etc. Parents are the most important role-models for their children. It is important that children don't feel that they are the only ones who are involved in reading; they should see an interest from adults too.
• Parents can be encouraged to continue reading to their children even if their children can read quite well on their own. Reading *to* children does

Let's see if we can find Auntie Maggie's phone number.

TELEPHONE DIRECTORY

not make them lazy about reading for themselves. It enables them to have all the benefits of a reading experience without the effort and it stimulates a greater interest in reading.
• They can be encouraged to use a local library or, if the local library is not local enough, they can use the school library to browse among the books with their children and to share in the choice of books.
• They can be encouraged to buy books for their children from jumble sales, car boot sales or book shops. They could consider giving a special book as a present for a birthday or Christmas.
• They can be encouraged to give their children a book allowance. This can be part of the usual pocket money but specifically designated to be spent on books.
• Between the ages of seven and twelve, many children develop hobbies, such as cycling, gymnastics, fishing, dancing, computers, etc. Often parents are involved in their children's hobbies, if only

because they have to ferry them about to various venues! These hobbies and interests can be a good opportunity for parents and children to share reading interests, either in the form of a club magazine or specialist books.

How can parental involvement be encouraged?

It is up to schools to make opportunities to convey the importance of parents' responsibility towards their child's development as an independent reader. There are a number of approaches that can be taken.
• Hold a book week, involving parents as much as possible. For valuable information about running a book week, including

authors/illustrators to invite to school, contact Book Trust (see Resources, page 192).
• Hold a storytelling week and invite parents to attend.
• Keep a reading diary with space for the child, teacher and parent to make comments (see photocopiable page 185).
• Some parents might welcome the opportunity to assist in the day-to-day running of the school library.
• Copy and distribute photocopiable page 186, which outlines advice for parents.

What about those children who find reading difficult?

Some parents feel their child's progress in reading seems frustratingly slow, even though the school may be doing all it can to bolster the child's confidence and to provide specific support in reading. Over the years, teachers have built up considerable expertise in how best to help these children, but for most parents it is their first experience of having to provide such support and consequently they are often at a loss to know what to do. Without guidance from the school these parents will only increase their children's problems, either by making them anxious or by backing off and doing nothing. It is important to be very sympathetic to these genuine parental concerns. There are three possible ways to address them.
• Do not fob off parents with comments like, 'Don't worry, it will be all right eventually.' Even if time is all that is needed to remedy the

problem, parents will find such advice very difficult to accept. Instead, point out the child's strengths, for example, what she can do now that she could not do three months before. Explain the aspects of reading the child finds difficult. Give details about what the school is doing and what the school would like them to do to support the child.

Photocopiable pages 179 and 180 show a child's initial skills, developing skills and attitude to reading. This may be a very useful basis for such a discussion.
• Share with parents some of the resources that the school is using to support the child, for example, word recognition games and word rhyming games. Parents often have the time to play such games with their children at home.
• Enlist parents' help to keep alive their children's interest in reading and books. Lend them story tapes to share together at

home; lend them picture books to share – such books are fun to pore over but the reluctant reader need not be daunted by chunks of text that are difficult to decode. Photocopiable page 187 recommends some picture books for juniors.

The Parents' Charter (DES, 1991) tells parents, 'As parents, the biggest help you can give to your child is to show that you are interested and see the value of what he or she is doing at school. Such support can have a real effect on your child's performance – and on his or her future.'

As teachers we need to provide the structure for this parental support.

Perhaps you and Natasha might like to listen to this together. It's a collection of animal stories.

CHAPTER 17

Assessment and record-keeping

The roots of assessment

Many people are surprised to discover that assessment only began in the nineteenth century. The industrial revolution meant large numbers of people left the countryside and flocked into the towns, so the need to select and train professional people became increasingly apparent. The first to recognise this were the doctors who instigated qualifying exams in 1815. In 1850 the Oxford and Cambridge Examination board was established. This was the first board to try to offer university places according to intellectual ability rather than solely on the ability to pay the fees. Thus the original basis of assessment was to help identify the intelligence of potential students.

In 1904 the Minister of Public Instruction in Paris asked Alfred Binet to construct a test which would distinguish between those children who should be educated in ordinary schools and those who should not. The test he devised became known as the Stanford-Binet test and it has been in continuous use since that date. The IQ test was developed by Burt in 1913 who used the test to select those children who were in need of 'special education'.

BACKGROUND

The idea of assessment as a means of selecting the appropriate education developed rapidly and in 1926 the Hadow Report suggested that all children should receive secondary education, but not all of the same type. Some would benefit from an academic education and should attend a grammar school, while others should go to a secondary modern school. By 1944 the eleven plus exam was firmly in place and children were assessed on English, arithmetic and intelligence. This form of assessment was not intended to demean children – rather it was to ensure they received the most appropriate education, based upon equality of opportunity. However, there was an increasing feeling that these ideals were not being achieved. The eleven plus exam was shown to favour white middle class Anglo-Saxon children, many of whom were coached for the exam.

From the 1970's onwards the emphasis on assessment and the place it should play began to change. In the primary schools, particularly, teachers began to ask for assessment to provide a great deal more than just a graded list of pupils provided by a written test taken at a specific time on a certain day. The establishment of the National Curriculum has underlined the need for careful monitoring and assessment based upon teacher records and standardised assessment tasks.

Why assess?

TGAT's stated purposes for assessment were:
• formative – it should emphasise what the pupil has achieved and help to identify where the pupil could go next with any set task;
• diagnostic – it should help to identify what kind of help is appropriate for any individuals;
• summative – it should describe the overall progress of the pupil;
• evaluative – it should contain information on 'how well' the school is doing and this information should be available to parents, governors, local education authorities and the DES.

SEAC wanted to take this further and suggested the main reason for any assessment is to INFORM:
Identify statements of attainment in lesson plans;
Note opportunities for children to demonstrate learning;
Focus on performance as evidence of attainment;
Offer children the chance to discuss what was achieved;
Record noteworthy items of observation and discussion;
Modify subsequent lesson plans in the light of the records.

The result of this change in emphasis can be summarised in the 'assessment cycle'. Teachers need to *plan* their teaching carefully so that it matches the needs of the individual child as closely as possible; in order to do this they have to *observe* what the child can do and to *review* this information so that they can more effectively *plan* their teaching.

How can we assess reading?

As our understanding of the complexity of the reading process deepens, so it is essential that our assessment reflects this knowledge. It is no longer acceptable to administer a 'reading test' once a year in order to monitor a pupil's progress and to believe that this gives an adequate picture of the child as a reader. Nor is it acceptable to describe reading as 'weak', 'good' and so on. The example below undoubtedly took the teacher some time to compose and write, and yet it provides no real knowledge as to Louise's reading ability.

'Louise has made good progress with her reading but she does need plenty of practice in order to maintain this progress.'

We now have to assess the process as well as the product and it is only by *observing* the child's attitude, *listening* to the child read, *discussing* what he has read and his *response* to the text that we can begin to get anything like an accurate picture of a child's reading ability.

Who is the assessment for?

Until recently, reading assessment was usually monitored by the administration of a published standardised test. It was seen as something required by the headteacher, who was generally required to do this by her local authority, who presumably could send this information to the DES. However, in practice, these kinds of records can't have got much further than the headteacher's desk as so few authorities could produce any reliable evidence of reading standards in their county when the whole question of a 'fall' in standards was thrust into the limelight by the revelations of Martin Turner in 1990.

The results of assessment in its fullest form should be made available to all concerned with the child. This will include the present teacher, the headteacher, the child and the child's carer, and the child's next teacher. A whole-school policy of assessment which informs all these parties is essential. For far too long the child has been left out of his own assessment and very few children have any idea of what they are seeking to achieve. The teacher needs to make explicit to all the children in her care what she expects from them. This information needs also to be shared with the child's carer.

Any assessment must be clearly understood by the child's next teacher and any information has to be simple, accurate and informative. The language used to describe and record a child's reading behaviour, strategies and responses need to be agreed and understood by the whole staff. Therefore a school policy with which all teachers are familiar is essential.

Finally, the local or central

authority is likely to need assurance that an assessment policy is in place, and although the SAT results are one form of evidence it is likely that these will need to be supported by observational records.

Managing assessment

The major problem that teachers face is that fuller records shared with more individuals take up more time. Many teachers feel that this has become an overwhelming problem, the result of which has taken away teaching time from the child. However, teachers would agree that keeping information in the memory is neither effective nor useful. Teachers have to make time in the school day for collecting evidence of achievement and recording that information for others. Consider the following ways of saving time during the day:

• Are there any routine classroom procedures which could be revised or abandoned? For example, when taking the school register, is it really necessary for each child to respond, 'Good morning, Mrs So-and-so'? Could some of the day-to-day tasks be taken over by the children, such as keeping the book corner tidy, stocked, administered, and so on.
• Look at the way the physical space is organised and try alternative ways of storing, allowing easier access to resources.
• Ensure that the children realise there are times when you need to write and record without interruption.
• Involve the children in their own evaluation and recording.
• Have a simple format for recording that all teachers know how to use as part of school policy.
• Set aside a regular time, perhaps once a term, to have an in-depth reading interview with each child, recording reading behaviour, strategies and responses.

As teachers become more at ease with assessment it is likely to become much easier, and any activity that takes place will add to knowledge of the child and, therefore, become part of the assessment process.

Collecting evidence

You will need evidence to back up your assessments, but what form should this take? Consider what counts as evidence.
• Is a list of books a child has read, written on to a piece of card, sufficiently informative?
• Is it important to note how long it has taken for a child to complete a book?
• Is it important for you to know how a reader responded to a book?
• How important is it for you to keep a taped reading of a story or a page marked for miscues?
• Is it necessary to keep a record of a child's response to what has been read?
• Do you need to know accurately the strategies a child is able to use?

(NB For further information about this kind of assessment, the ILEA Language Record has been recognised as a

The cover's a bit boring isn't it?

Well I like it because....

worthwhile and useful form of reading assessment.)

Many teachers feel that they do not wish to spend their time ticking boxes; indeed, they argue very convincingly that one tick in a box is quite inadequate and lots of filled boxes fail to give anything like as accurate a picture as a five-minute chat at lunch time. Some teachers have suggested various ways of recording achievement within the box to show how far the 'skill' has been internalised, for example, a diagonal line, a cross or the box hatched in. Others have wanted to record how frequently a task has been 'visited' as it is unlikely that real consolidation can be achieved by one exposure. When considering such issues, the whole staff need to be consulted and the primary aim should be simplicity coupled with accuracy. Photocopiable pages 188 and 189 offer suggestions for simple recording and assessment sheets.

Is there a place for the standard reading test?

Although the published tests are no longer considered adequate on their own, in many schools they still form a significant part in overall assessment of a child's progress. If these are to be used, it is essential that the school recognises the extent of the information they provide. It is rare for a standardised test to target more than one or two areas of the reading process.

Unfortunately there is no evidence to show us which is the 'best' model for these tests. Some use a multiple choice approach where the reader is offered a selection of words from which to choose the most appropriate, others use a cloze procedure in which the reader is supposed to provide the missing word for a selected 'gap' using context clues, while others may give a list of words which have been graded for difficulty for the reader to 'read'.

What these tests do offer is an unbiased record of how the child performs a limited task on a particular day. They can help the teacher evaluate the effectiveness of her teaching for that task and they are a way of judging the children's performance against a national standard. Many teachers use them in order to be reassured that their class is performing to the national average.

What is meant by a norm-referenced test?

These tests compare children with the 'norm'. The point is to demonstrate the difference between children. The results are often expressed in 'reading ages' so that teachers and parents quickly judge how the child is performing against the national average. However, such tests rarely give an indication as to why a test result is as it is. The role of these tests is only as good as the decisions made as a result of them. Those decisions should never stand in isolation but be related to professional judgements.

What is a criterion referenced test?

These tests compile information about a child in relation to mastery of a specific set of skills. Again, these tests are only as good as the set of sub-skills that they represent. They imply that children should have acquired a certain number of skills, generally in a certain order, at certain times in their life.

The National Curriculum is based on such a concept. For instance, it is expected that an average child of seven should have mastered the skills as described in the Statement of Attainment for Level 2 in reading. However, teachers appreciate that real reading is not so easily compartmentalised.

'Children do not learn particular features of reading once and for all at any particular stage; they continually return to the same features and refine their competence.' (The Cox Report. English 5-11 Nov 1988)

Considerations for assessing standardised tests

• Does the test reflect the philosophy of the school's approach to teaching reading?
• What does the test claim to measure and is this something the school considers to be of value?
• Is the content of the test interesting and relevant to the pupils? Does it take into account the multi-ethnic make-up of our society?
• Is the text of sufficient length to allow the reader to make use of a meaningful context?
• Will the test help the teacher to teach reading more effectively?
• In terms of both time and money, does the school consider the test worth the amount?
• When was the test first published?
• What is the age range that the test is aimed at? (Remember the wider the age range, the less accurate the information is likely to be.)
• What procedures were used for standardisation?

Informal observation of reading

'Observation is rarely good in any field unless the observer has a clear idea of what might be noticed and how that fits into the general context.' (Gipps, C. 1990)

The following is a brief list of things that schools might like to consider when planning what aspects of reading should be recorded for the child who is an independent reader. Children should not necessarily demonstrate all the aspects suggested.

Attitude to reading

• Enjoys silent reading periods.
• Has favourite authors.
• Enjoys group reading.
• Selects confidently from book corner/library.
• Rereads favourite books.
• Wants to tell others about 'good' reads.
• Has the confidence to reject some books.
• Reads books written on many levels.
• Likes sharing new knowledge.

Skills of the independent reader

• Able to retell plot clearly.
• Can discuss characters.
• Predicts plots based on careful reading.
• Uses intonation when reading aloud.
• Reads from many genres.
• Justifies choice/rejection.
• Can get information from non-fiction.
• Knows the significance of typefaces.
• Can scan texts for specific information.
• Can discuss inferential meaning.
• Self-corrects when reading aloud.
• Uses book knowledge across the curriculum.
• Knows the difference between fact and opinion.
• Keeps and uses own record.

PHOTOCOPIABLES

The pages in this section can be photocopied and adapted to suit your own needs and those of your class. They do not need to be declared in respect of any photocopying licence. Each photocopiable page relates to a specific activity or suggestion in the main body of the book and the appropriate activity and page references are given above each photocopiable sheet.

Certificate of merit, page 22

This certificate is presented to

in recognition of valuable help given in the upkeep of the school library.

Signed..............................

152 Photocopiable pages

Pathways, page 125

Going to school

Photocopiable pages 169

Child's reading record, page 149

Photocopiable pages 189

This certificate is presented to

in recognition of valuable help given in the upkeep of the school library.

Signed...........................

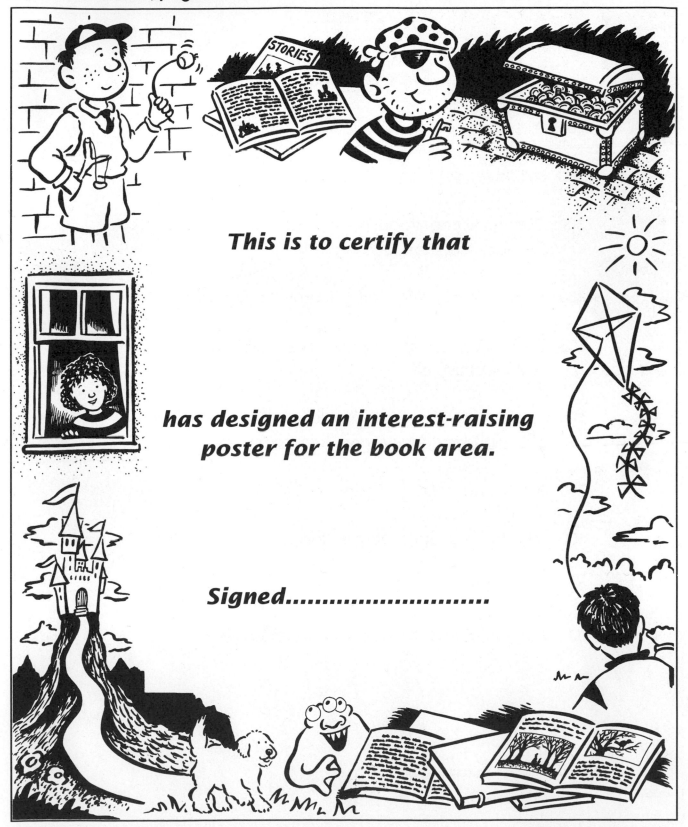

This is to certify that

has designed an interest-raising poster for the book area.

Signed............................

Dewey system

100 Philosophy, psychology, information

200 Beliefs, religions, mythologies

300 Community eg. trade, government, welfare, education, law, fairy tales, lore and legends

400 Language eg. dictionaries, thesauri, grammars

500 Science eg. natural history, mathematics, astronomy, physics, chemistry

600 Applied science and technology eg. human biology, cooking, pets, engineering, farming, inventions

700 Sport, recreation

800 Literature eg. plays, poetry, stories,

900 Geography, history, biography

00 Multi-subject books eg. encyclopaedias

Name: _____

Alias: _____

Age: _____

Address: _____

_____

_____

Major goal in life: _____

_____

_____

_____

_____

Name
Title of book

Characters	First impression	Second impression	Reason for change

Some of these characteristics might help you:

happy, unhappy, friendly, unfriendly, kind, cruel, brave, cowardly, tidy, messy, generous, mean, strong, weak, good, bad, smart, unlucky, intelligent, stupid, calm, excited, gentle, violent, timid, bombastic.

Character grid, page 72

Book title_____ Names in group_____

Author_____   _____

Character	Characteristic						

You may wish to select characteristics from the following list:

kind, cruel, friendly, happy, cheeky, loyal, brave, honest, timid, bossy, strong, weak, gentle, honest, sensible, proud, rude, silly, stupid, clever, calm, generous, mean, polite.

What did you think? page 73

	Name of book:
Character you would most like to meet	
Character you would least like to meet	
Character you would most like to be	
Character you would least like to be	
Most realistic character	
Least realistic character	
Characters similar to one in another book	
Characters unlike any from another book	
Characters' names	

Story map game for _____   Devised by _____

_____   _____

Write a reference, page 74

_______________ has applied for the job of _______________________

and has suggested that you would write a reference. Please include details of why you think this candidate should be considered and brief details concerning his/her punctuality, intelligence and attitude to work.

The information given above is true to the best of my knowledge.

Signed _______________

Date _____________

Reading diary, page 78

Date	Title	Author	Genre	Comment

'Hold your noise!' cried a terrible voice, as a man started up from among the graves at the side of the church porch. 'Keep still, you little devil, or I'll cut your throat!'

   A fearful man, all in coarse grey with a .... iron on his leg. A man with .... hat, and with .... shoes, and with an old .... tied round his head. A man who had been .... in water, and .... in mud, and .... by stones, and .... by flints, and .... by nettles and .... by briars; who limped, and ...., and glared and ....; and whose teeth .... in his head as he seized me by the chin.

(From Chapter One of *Great Expectations* by Charles Dickens)

Name _____

Characters	Setting
_____	_____
_____	_____
_____	_____
_____	_____
_____	_____
_____	_____
_____	_____

Complication	Ending
_____	_____
_____	_____
_____	_____
_____	_____
_____	_____
_____	_____

Title _____ Name _____

Character

Setting

First episode	Second episode	Third episode

Conclusion

'Go to bed,' said ....

It was morning at last

But that's another story

She found herself
back in her
room

'I've heard that before,' said her aunt

He fell over the edge

Just then, the mysterious noise started again!

Little Red Riding Hood

Fill in the blank boxes with caption texts

School report, page 111

Name ______________________ Form ____________

Age ______________________ Term ____________

General class behaviour		Grade
English		
Mathematics		
Science		
History/ Geography		
Music		
PE		

Grades A: Excellent B: Good C: Average D: Could do better

Signed ______________________________ Class teacher

Title of book _____

Name of character _____

	5	4	3	2	1	
good						bad
kind						unkind
generous						mean
good-tempered						bad-tempered
careful						careless
considerate						thoughtless
obedient						disobedient
honest						dishonest
happy						sad
understanding						cantankerous
sensible						silly

Character score:_____

CROESO

Welsh

স্বাগতম্

Bengali

ભલે પધાર્યા

Gujarati

स्वागतम्

Hindi

Punjabi

HOŞ GELDINIZ

Turkish

歡迎你

Chinese

Arabic

خوش آمدید

Urdu

BIENVENUS

French

Going to school

How do you and your friend get to school?

Ask your friend to draw your route on the map.

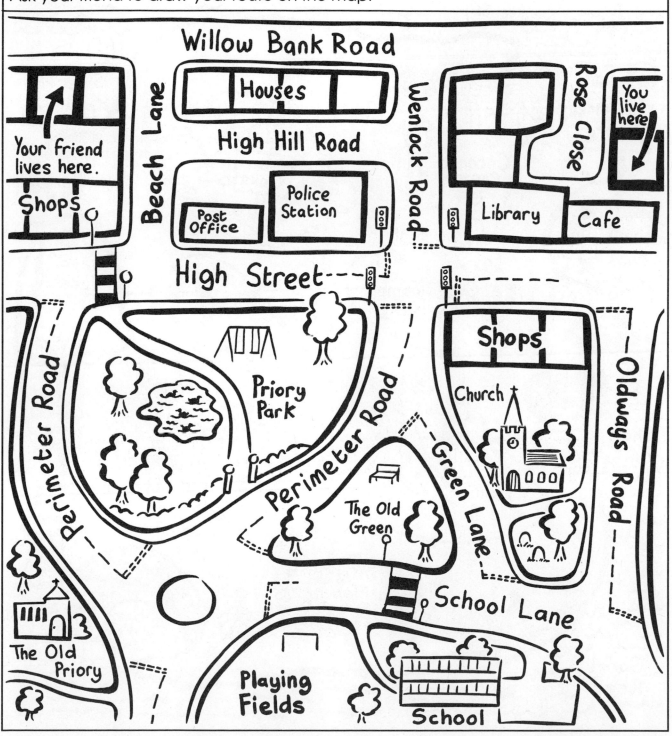

Choose your way.

Ask your friend how you will reach Rescue Harbour.

Spot the difference, page 129

What's wrong in this classroom?

Cloze procedure (one in twelve words)

The Old Lion

There once was a very old lion. As he grew older he found he
could ....catch his food. He decided to trick the animals
and make .... come to him.

So he went to the back of his .... and pretended to be
ill. Every day different animals came to .... how he was.

When they entered his cave he sprang on them and
.... them up.

One day a clever fox came to .... on the lion. The
fox did not go into the cave, ... called out, 'How
are you today, Mr Lion?'

'I am very ....,' said the lion. 'Why don't you
come in and see ....?'

'I would have done,' said the fox, 'if I hadn't noticed all
.... footprints point towards your cave and none the
other way!'

Cloze procedure (selected verbs deleted)

The Night the Wind Blew

As darkness fell, the wind began to blow over the hills. It rattled the tiles in the roof of the old farmhouse and .... the smoke back down the chimney. It .... up the loose straw that lay scattered in the farmyard.

The hens inside the barn .... in fright and the farm cat .... and yawned. Perhaps it .... time to see what was going on. There might be mice .... around the farmyard or even a rat to catch. The cat .... around the great doors of the barn and .... into the yard. The wind continued to blow the straw, but nothing else seemed to be moving. Just then the moon .... out from behind the clouds. Standing by the gate .... a large red fox. It was looking towards the hen house. Its tail .... down but the tiny white tip was slowly moving from side to side. The cat .... and waited. A gust of wind gathered up more loose straw and .... it up into the air and against the windows of the farmhouse. The cat .... the light come on in the farmer's bedroom and he knew the hens were safe. Then, just as it had come, the wind .... The straw floated back down into the yard. The cat stared, the fox ....., also gone as silently as he had...............

Idiomatic match, page 132

Put your skates on	Hurry up
Pull your socks up	Work harder
Toe the line	Do as you are told
That was a close shave	That was nearly an accident
All hands on deck	Everybody must help
A piece of cake	That was easy to do
Stop taking the mickey	Stop teasing
You can't see the wood for the trees	You are too involved in details and not the main things
He is not yet out of the woods	He is still in a dangerous situation
Make it snappy	Hurry up and do it quickly
Use your loaf	Think!
You're driving me up the wall	You are making me angry
Put your back into it	Make more effort
Your back to the wall	You have a great problem
Not taking a blind bit of notice	Taking absolutely no notice

Idiomatic match, page 132

All that glitters is not gold	Things can appear better than they are
Too many cooks spoil the broth	Too many people involved are not helpful
A stitch in time saves nine	Doing something immediately saves time later
Many hands make light work	If everybody helps, the work doesn't seem so bad
You don't miss the water until the well dries up	You don't appreciate what you have until you lose it
A man with one eye is king among the blind	You may have lost something, but there are others worse off than you
A nod is as good as a wink to a blind man	There is no need to say anything more about it
Don't put all your eggs into one basket	Don't rely on only one thing
Don't count your chickens before they are hatched	Wait until you are certain before you act on something

Reading checklist, page 136

Reading checklist	Always	Sometimes	Never
Attitude			
* listens to stories with obvious enjoyment			
* chooses to listen to stories on tape			
* likes looking at books during quiet reading time			
* talks about stories			
* enjoys looking at illustrations			
* is confident enough to reject a book			
* takes pride in books read alone			
* likes to know what happens at the end of a story			
* has an interest in specific reading eg. fishing			
* appears less anxious when asked to read to an adult			
Initial skills			
* recognises own name			
* points to where a reader should start to read			
* knows the meaning of the terms: word; letter; title; author			
* knows the direction of print			
* recognises some individual words in context			
* recognises and name some letters and attaches relevant sounds			
* predicts what might happen next in a story			
* joins in rhyming words			
* can write some words from memory			
* can retell a story in own words			

Developing skills	Always	Sometimes	Never
* can read environmental signs and notices			
* can name letters of the alphabet and knows alphabetical order			
* uses letter sounds to help decode unknown words			
* is developing a sight vocabulary			
* begins to tackle both fiction and non-fiction texts			
* joins in group reading			
* has the confidence to re-read texts			
* can sequence into logical order both fiction and non-fiction texts			

Cloze that space, page 139

There once were .... cats of Kilkenny
Each thought there were one .... too ....
So they fought and they fit
And they scratched and they ....
Till, excepting their nails
And the tips of their ....
Instead of .... cats there weren't any.

Burp!

There once was a lady .... Riga
Who went for a .... on a tiger
They returned from the ride
With the lady ....
And a smile on the .... of the tiger.

There was a young .... of Leeds
Who swallowed a .... of seeds
It soon came to pass
He was covered in ....
And couldn't sit .... for the weeds.

Mastermind, page 139

Subject _____ Devised by _____ Circle your answer			
	Is this true? A	Is this true? B	Is this true? C	
Fact 1.			A B C
Fact 2			A B C
Fact 3			A B C

The correct answers are: _____

_____

Title of book _____   Author _____

Characters:

_____

_____

_____

_____

_____

_____

Place names:

_____

_____

_____

_____

_____

_____

Write a review, page 140

1. Author _____ 2. Title _____

3. Publisher _____ 4. ISBN_____

5. Use this list to decide what type of book it is and highlight the words: a story about animals, families, sport, relationships, school, mystery, ghost, humour, adventure, fantasy, science-fiction, fairy story, going back in time, choose-your-own-adventure, solve the mystery, poetry, war, short-stories/annuals.

6. What is the book about?_____

_____

7. Which characters did you like and/or dislike the most?_____

_____

8. If you enjoyed the book, select words from the list which describes it and circle them: exciting, funny, believable characters, lots of action, unusual twists and turns, a good ending, an understandable story line, true to life, words used were interesting, good illustrations, print size was easy to read.

9. If you did not enjoy the book, select words from the list which describe it best and circle them: slow moving, too predictable, difficult to follow, characters were not believable, ending was weak, difficult to get into, words were difficult to understand, slow to get started, too long, too far fetched, not enough illustrations, words were printed too small.

10. Give this book a mark out of ten _____

11. I started this book on _____ and finished it on_____

12. The book came from: the school library, the class library, a friend, a relative, bookshop, the public library.

Reading diary, page 143

Name _____

Reading record

Date	Title	Child's/Carer's comment	Teacher's comment	Strategies used	Where next?

Advice for parents

• Keep shared reading times as relaxed as possible. If your child does not want to read to you, you read to him.

• When your children are reading to you and they come to a word that they cannot read you might like to try some of the following tactics:

1. You read the words which lead up to the unknown word. Sometimes that gives the child a clue to the missing word. They are then able to read it for themselves.

2. Suggest your child reads on further as later words might be clues to the missing word.

     If neither of these prompts helps, then tell your child what the word is. Also, to maintain the flow of the story, it is a good idea if *you* reread the sentence, page or paragraph up to the point where they stumbled.

• The most important thing is to encourage your child to read for meaning. If they make a mistake gently suggest that the reason why it is wrong is because it does not make sense.

• If what your child has read makes good sense but it is not exactly the word used in the book, it is not always essential to correct him or her. For example, if your child reads, 'I am putting on my socks,' and the actual words are, 'I am pulling on my socks,' there is no point in correcting the mistake. The mistakes that matter are the ones when what is read does not make sense.

• Talk about the author of the book. Try to remember if you have had other books by the same author.

• Your child will have favourite stories he or she will want to read over and over again. It is best just to go along with this need.

• Make sure your child sees you reading. This does not have to be a long novel – newspapers, letters, recipe books and magazines are all important variations of everyday reading material.

• Take your child to the library and choose books together. Sometimes your child will choose books you might not have selected, but learning about choosing books is all part of being a reader.

• Don't be tempted to test your child's knowledge of individual words.

Share a book with your child. Try one of the following titles:

Animalia, Graeme Base (Macmillan).

The Boy with Square Eyes, C. and J. Snape (Julia MacRae).

Dracula's Bedtime Storybook, Victor Ambrus (Oxford University Press).

The Great Green Mouse Disaster, Martin Waddell and Philippe Dupasquier (Beaver Books).

Little Dracula's First Bite, Martin Waddell (Walker Books).

Magical Changes, Graham Oakley (Macmillan).

Round Trip, Ann Jonas (Julia MacRae).

Stanley Bagshaw and the Short-sighted Football Trainer, Bob Wilson (Puffin).

War and Peas, Michael Foreman (Puffin).

Where's Wally?, Martin Handford (Walker Books).

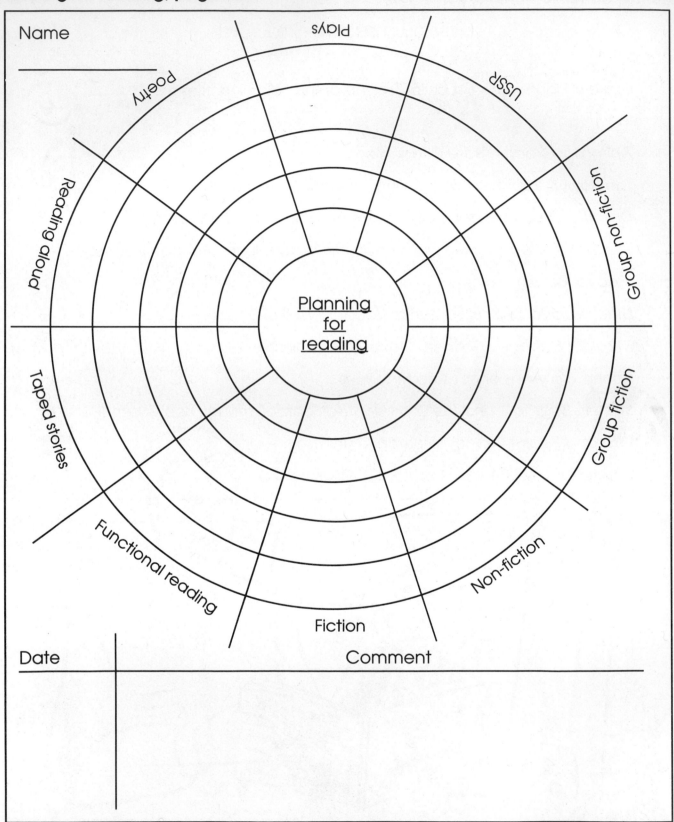

Name

Date

Comment

Planning
for
reading

Plays

USSR

Group non-fiction

Group fiction

Non-fiction

Fiction

Functional reading

Taped stories

Reading aloud

Poetry

My own reading record

England and Wales

The chart on this page refers to the reading component of the National Curriculum for English. Use this chart to identify the chapters that support each statement of attainment.

Level	Chapter	1	2	3	4	5	6	7	8	9	10	11	12	13	14	15
2	a											*		*		
	b	*			*											
	c														*	*
	d								*		*				*	*
	e		*	*				*		*						*
	f	*		*					*							*
3	a					*		*					*			
	b								*							
	c		*					*		*	*		*			*
	d	*		*		*		*		*	*					
	e			*				*			*	*	*		*	*
	f		*		*							*				
4	a			*		*		*					*			
	b	*	*	*				*			*			*		
	c			*		*	*	*		*	*			*	*	
	d	*	*		*						*					
5	a			*		*		*		*						
	b	*		*		*				*	*			*		
	c				*		*							*		
	d	*	*		*											
	e			*	*	*					*					

Scotland

The chart on this page refers to the reading component of the Scottish curriculum for English language. Use this chart to identify the strands covered by the activities in this book. Activities are identified by their chapter and activity numbers; for example, **4**/1 means Chapter 4, activity 1.

Level / Strand	B	C	D	E
Reading for information	**2**/3, **2**/5, **4**/1-2, **13**/1, **14**/1-2, **14**/6-11, **15**/4-5	**2**/3, **2**/5, **4**/1-2, **4**/4-7, **13**/1-2, **13**/8-9, **14**/1-2, **14**/6-11, **15**/4-5	**2**/3, **4**/1-3, **4**/4-7, **13**/1-2, **13**/8-9, **15**/4-5	**4**/2-3, **4**/4-7, **13**/1-2, **13**/8-9
Reading for enjoyment	**1**/1, **1**/5, **3**/8, **5**/1-5, **10**/1-7, **12**/6-7, **14**/12, **15**/2	**1**/1, **1**/5, **3**/8, **5**/1-5, **7**/6, **10**/1-8, **12**/6-7, **14**/12, **15**/2	**1**/1, **1**/5, **3**/4, **3**/8, **5**/1-5, **7**/6, **10**/1-9, **12**/6-7, **15**/2	**1**/1, **1**/5, **3**/4, **3**/8, **5**/1-5, **7**/6, **10**/1-9, **12**/6-7
Reading to reflect on the writer's ideas and craft	**1**/2, **2**/4, **3**/1-2, **3**/5, **3**/8, **5**/1, **5**/3-7, **10**/1-7, **11**/1-5, **12**/1-7, **13**/3-10, **14**/12-16, **15**/1-3, **15**/6	**1**/2, **2**/4, **3**/1-8, **5**/1, **5**/3-7, **6**/3-5, **7**/1-6, **10**/1-8, **11**/1-5, **12**/1-7, **13**/3-10, **14**/12-16, **15**/1-3, **15**/6	**1**/2, **2**/4, **3**/1-8, **5**/1, **5**/3-7, **6**/3-5, **7**/1-6, **10**/1-9, **11**/1-5, **12**/1-7, **13**/3-10, **14**/12-16, **15**/2-3, **15**/6	**1**/2, **2**/4, **3**/1-8, **5**/1, **5**/3-7, **6**/3-5, **7**/1-6, **10**/1-9, **11**/1-5, **12**/1-7, **13**/3-10
Awareness of genre (type of text)	**1**/3-4, **5**/6-7, **11**/1-5, **12**/4-5, **13**/5, **14**/1-2, **15**/8	**1**/3-4, **4**/6, **5**/6-7, **6**/1-5, **11**/1-5, **12**/4-5, **13**/5, **14**/1-2, **15**/8	**1**/3-4, **4**/6, **5**/6-7, **6**/1-5, **11**/1-5, **12**/4-5, **13**/5, **14**/1-2, **15**/8	**1**/3-4, **4**/6, **5**/6-7, **6**/1-5, **11**/1-5, **12**/4-5, **13**/5
Reading aloud				
Knowledge about language	**1**/3, **2**/1, **3**/5-6, **5**/8, **14**/1, **14**/3-10, **14**/14, **14**/16, **15**/3, **15**/7	**1**/3, **2**/1, **3**/5-6, **5**/8, **6**/4, **10**/8, **11**/1, **11**/5, **12**/2, **14**/1, **14**/3-10, **14**/14, **14**/16, **13**/3, **15**/7	**1**/3, **2**/1-2, **3**/5-6, **5**/8, **6**/4, **10**/8, **11**/1, **11**/5, **12**/2, **14**/14, **14**/16, **15**/3	**1**/3, **2**/1-2, **3**/5-6, **5**/8, **6**/4, **10**/8, **11**/5, **12**/2

Resources

Books for Keeps, 6 Brightfield Road, Lee, London SE12 8QF.

Letterbox Library, Freepost, 8 Bradbury Street, London N16 8BR.

Puffin Book Club, Freepost, 27 Wrights Lane, London W8 5BR.

Scholastic Book Clubs, Westfield Road, Southam, Leamington Spa CV33 0JH.

The Children's Book Foundation, Book House Trust, 45 East Hill, London SW18 2QZ.

Altair Design, Longman Group UK Ltd, Longman House, Burnt Mill, Harlow, Essex CM20 2JE.

Bibliography

Bentley, D. et al (1992) *Inspirations for Becoming a Reader*, Scholastic.

Chambers, A. (1985) *Book Talk*, Bodley Head.

Chambers, A. (1991) *The Reading Environment*, Thimble Press.

Charles, C.M. (1980) *Individual Instruction*, C.V. Moshy.

Clark-Sayers, F. (1973) *Summoned by Books*, Viking.

DES (1988) *Report of the Committee of Enquiry into the Teaching of English Language* (The Kingman Report), HMSO.

Goodman, K. (1976) 'Reading: a psycholinguistic guessing game' in *Theoretical Models and Processes of Reading*, ed. A. Singer and R.B. Ruddell Newark, International Reading Association.

Halliday, M. (1975) *Learning how to Mean – Explorations in the Development of Meaning*, Edward Arnold.

Hughes, T. (1963) *Listening to Poetry*, Hutchinson.

Johnson (1973) *Reading, Teaching and Learning*, Macmillan.

Lunzer and Gardner (1979) *The Effective Use of Reading*, Heinemann.

Meek, M. (1991) *On Being Literate*, Bodley Head.

Moon (1991) *Assessing Reading at Key Stage 1*, University of Reading.

Ousbey, J. (1987) 'Taking care of the small box' in *Books for Keeps*, November 1987.

Southgate, V. et al (1976) *Extending Beginning Reading*, Heinemann Educational.

Watts, I. (1811) *The Improvement of the Mind*.

Computer programs

Developing Tray, ILECC, John Ruskin Street, London SE5 0PQ.

Front Page Extra, MESU, Sir William Lyons Road, Science Park, University of Warwick, Coventry CV4 7EZ.

News Bulletin, Newman Software Ltd, Newman College, Bartley Green, Birmingham B32 3NT.